"We shall not cease from exploration. And the end of all our exploring will be to arrive where we started and know the place for the first time." **T.S. Eliot**

Introduction

My sister Shushie and I are no strangers to the Coast to Coast walk. This was to be the third time we'd crossed the northern part of the UK on foot.

Our first outing began in 1997 when Shushie was newly single and living in the north east, within striking distance of the walk's official finishing line at Robin Hood's Bay. I was married with two children and living back in the town where we'd grown up – Milton Keynes. But it was our complicated lives that separated us more than the 200-mile drive.

Which meant it took our years of snatched weekends before we'd completed the 190 miles of the Coast to Coast. And that first time we walked east from Robin Hood's Bay because a) it was closer to Shushie's home and therefore the logistics were easier to begin with, and b) because we were saving the best – our beloved Lake District – for last.

By October 2000, when we reached St Bees Head on the west coast, the end of the walk, I was living apart from my husband and Shushie had come south to live with a new partner. Instead of the walk being a way in which we could reconnect with each other the Coast to Coast had become a shared escape route. It was what we did whenever we felt the need to retreat, regroup and reimagine our lives.

So there was no question we needed to continue. In 2002, after a two-year break, we decided to simply turn around and retrace our steps from St Bees' Head across the Lakes, through the lush Dales and, via the switchback of the Cleveland Hills to the Yorkshire Moors and back down to the sea.

It took us another four years and once again, by the time we were done, the landscape of our lives was as different from when we'd started as the scenery we had walked through.

The midsummer's day, in 2006, when we returned to Robin's Hood Bay, ought to have been a time of celebration and satisfaction. We had, in the words of *The Hobbit*, been there and back again. We had walked through death, disappointment and despair, but also through hope and faith and change, buoyed by humour and each other's support.

Instead, we felt only sadness at the loss of something to which so much of ourselves had somehow become attached. Slogging through the watershed at the very heart of the country; lost and very, very afraid in a storm at Kidsty Pike; skimming the edge of the Cleveland ridge ready to fly like birds: every memory of those two long walks told a story of who we'd been. If we stopped then we'd be ending the story of our lives too.

There was only one thing for it: a promise to ourselves and each other that, when the time was right, we would return.

So here we are. It is now April 26 2013. The gap has been far, far longer than either of us imagined. As have the challenges of the intervening years.

No matter; tomorrow we start moving again….and who knows where we will end up?

A word about blisters

The miles can be particularly unforgiving to very occasional walkers like Shushie and I. We've chalked up some fairly dramatic blisters and I'm quite sure we'll be sharing a few more in the coming months. But, if you'll excuse the Cockney rhyming slang, the blisters I'm really referring to are Shushie and I: skin and blisters.

2

And a word about the rest of our lives

We've been caring for our mum since November 2009, and I mention that in this introduction because, as any carer will tell you, it's the role that everything else has to fit itself around. It's not the first time we've been here either: we spent five years caring for mum's brother until he died of cancer in 2000.

That experience inspired me to write *The Carer's Handbook*, which opened the door to publishers, enabling me to at last fulfil a lifelong dream of being able to call myself a writer. More books followed.

The other elements of my rather random 'portfolio' life are coaching and leading workshops as a licenced facilitator of Louise Hay's *Heal Your Life* programmes – plus occasional freelance marketing and communications.

Random, as I said, but when has my life ever not been a work in progress?

As for Shushie, she's into healing too, more practically in her case, as practice nurse at a GPs' surgery.

About the Coast to Coast walk

Devised by Alfred Wainwright in 1973, theCoast to Coast walk is a 192 mile (293km) long distance route across northern England.

Though it's not an official walking route – and therefore not particularly well-signed – the Coast to Coast is actually the M25 of walks - apparently the most popular of the UK's long distance walks worldwide.

Its popularity may derive from its passage through no fewer than three national parks of outstanding beauty: the Lake District, Yorkshire Dales and North Yorks Moors.

But it is certainly enhanced by the fact that the entire walk fits neatly into the annual two weeks, conveniently divided into 12-14 sections, ranging in distance from 9-23 miles.

Since Wainwright put the walk on the map – literally – there have been countless guidebooks to help walkers navigate their way from St Bees Head on the Irish Sea, to Robin Hood's Bay on the North Sea. But there is no substitute for the original; Wainwright was quirky and curmudgeonly but the hills and dales were also the one great love of his life. Having his book in your rucksack is to have a great companion alongside, opinionated but hugely knowledgeable.

For the record, we're using the second edition, published in 2010 by Frances Lincoln.

We're also carrying the Cicerone Guide to *A Northern Coast to Coast Walk* by Terry Marsh, because it has a small but useful section at the back on doing the walk from east to west. And for reference at home, we've got Henry Stedman's *Coast to Coast Path*, from the British Walking Guide Series, and Ronald Turnbull's *Coast to Coast*, published by Dalesman.

The existence of so many excellent guides – of which these are only a few – explains why this account won't include specific guidance on directions, but focuses on our experience of *doing* the walk.

Before mum got ill our walking weekends were such an important part of our lives Shushie and I would be planning them into our diaries as soon as New Year's Day came around. After a massive stroke left her helpless as a kitten every aspect of our lives had to be altered to accommodate her care needs.

Any time away -especially together - had to be negotiated with a complicated system of paid support. But it wasn't 'arrangements' that tied our feet so much as classic carers' guilt about taking any time for ourselves that wasn't strictly necessary.

That lasted up to the point where we both recognized if we didn't

4

soon do something for ourselves we'd be the ones needing care. We were exhausted, stressed – and to be honest bored – by the relentlessness of lives determined by everyone's else's need for our support.

Living life now

One of my escapes, so long we were unable to continue our walking, were my books - among them, Sarah Ban Breathnach's beautiful *Simple Abundance*.

There was a passage that hit home, penetrating the fug of duty and routine. She writes: "There are three ways to change the trajectory of our lives: crisis, chance and choice."

Conscious choice is creative, the heart of authenticity, she believes, whereas unconscious choice is living the way other people expect us to, or the way we *believe* they need or want us to.

And of course we all know what crisis is…

That was when it dawned on me that no-one was going to give Shushie and I permission to save (at least a part of) our own lives by heading for the hills again. We had to be brave enough to do that for ourselves. I wrote in my journal:

'Last night I took a deep breath and talked to Shushie about walking the Coast to Coast again this year over six weekends. In her face I saw all my own objections: how can we possibly get away from our lives? There are so many reasons not to do it now; to postpone until we're no longer carers.

Yet if we wait will time and opportunity wait for us? Mum's deterioration is slow and I suspect we will be called on to dig deeper, to do more, and to cope for a long while yet.

So the decision to do it anyway, in the face of all the actual and imagined objections, all the guilt, all the logistical challenges, all the effort it will take to set things up so we might get away.

Our choice is to Live Life Now. Knowing that every journey happens both outside and within.

The fourth 'c' in Ban Breathnach's equation is 'change'. By the end of this year, when we reach the coast once again, it's a certainty that life will not be the same as it is starting out today.

Bring it on Change!

A little small print

It's some years now since I wrote the first draft of this book. In that time guest houses, hotels, restaurants, pubs and shops have come and gone, changed hands or changed out of all recognition.

Some of the best we encountered survived the years but if you're doing this walk (oh, lucky, lucky you…) please do check the latest information for yourselves. You might even want to blog about it so that when next my sis and I pass that way we can check out *your* recommendations.

Same message about the route: it changed very little for us over the course of the almost 20 years we were crossing backwards and forwards, but the National Parks authorities are very mindful of the damage our combined boots cause and sometimes steer Coast to Coasters steps a little away from Wainwright's original.

Chapter 1: The end? Robin Hood's Bay

Most walkers, I imagine, navigate the steep and very narrow road down through Robin Hood's Bay with a big grin on their weatherbeaten faces.

Unlike Shushie and I, who rather self-consciously are keeping our eyes firmly on the ground.

We're worried, you see, that the groups of tourists milling around shopfronts and the public toilets, might want to congratulate us on a job well done. If you are heading through the town to the beach, knees buckling under the weight of a fat rucksack, if your steps are accompanied by the metallic click of a walking stick, if your camera is in your hand: then, it stands to reason, you are on your way to completing Wainwright's epic Coast to Coast walk.

Which of course we aren't. Flying in the face of Wainwright's advice that west to east puts the prevailing winds firmly behind you – something we'll have good reason to remember over and over during the next two days – our walk is starting on the North Yorkshire coast…on a beach packed with dog walkers and a noisy school field trip and young families who've suffered six months of cabin fever and are dammed if a 40 mph wind whipping up sea foam is going to keep them inside a moment longer.

Even the ice cream van has come out to play… though in the half hour we sit on the sea wall, staring seawards with chattering teeth, he doesn't have a single customer.

We want to end in the Lakes, as we did the first time we walked across the country between 1997-2000. Then, because Shushie was living in Teeside so the logistics were easier. And this time because on a walk that truly winds its way through the very best England has to offer, Cumbria's purple hills and silent lakes represent the best of that best.

It's a British thing, I fear, saving the best for last. (Please reassure me that I'm not the only one who sometimes pushes food around on the plate saving the 'best' mouthful to the end?) Just as it feels a part of our national character to feel we don't deserve praise if it's not been earned the hard way: no pain no gain.

So it's a relief, finally walking out onto the beach beyond any danger of being fraudulently congratulated for an achievement that is not yet ours, and won't be for another seven or eight months – the time we intend this walk, over a series of weekends, to take.

We dip our toes in the North Sea, as Wainwright instructs, and then we each choose a small pebble to carry with us, buried in jacket pockets, until it can be safely delivered to the beach at St Bees on the Irish Sea. I'd like to think our two little pebbles going 'the wrong way' will go a little way to redressing the balance of stone and rock travelling in the other direction.

Barry was here: Robin Hood's Bay-Hawsker

Have I mentioned yet that walking there *and back* on the Coast to Coast took Shushie and I a less-than-impressive eight years the first time? Oh, alright then; I'm only bringing it up again because we've sometimes wondered whether we might hold the record for the slowest ever crossing of the country…

As opposed to a Mr Barry Pincer, who quite possibly achieved one of the fastest.

Our source for this nugget is the assistant serving in a tiny souvenir shop halfway up the hill out of Robin Hood's Bay. We'd popped in to buy a couple of Coast to Coast cloth badges. When we were children dad always used the promise of a cloth badge to lure us – then, far more interested in penny machines and donkey rides – up some serious Lakeland fells. It's a hard habit to break.

"You've finished the walk then have you girls?" the assistant says brightly.

"Well no. We're just starting out."

"Oh but then that's cheating."

Shushie jumps in before she can decide she oughtn't to sell us the badges, explaining this is not our first but our third Coast to Coast.

"Ah," she nods approvingly. "My friend does it in four days. He's done it loads of times. There and back. Four days – he doesn't stop you see. Walks day and night. I think he's doing it again this summer.

"Barry's his name. Barry Pincer."

For the record, Wainwright divides his walk into 12 sections and suggests that in reasonable weather it can be done in two weeks: "a very strong athlete might do it in a week, but this is a walk that ought to be done in comfort and for pleasure or not at all".

We pay and leave the shop without saying aloud what we're thinking: poor old Barry. He still thinks it's about getting there, when – if the walking has taught us one thing – it's that it's all about the journey. Miss what's under your nose every step of the way and you miss the whole point.

A gift of a day

On this first leg, for instance, what's under our noses is the sort of assault on the senses that only the first real spring day after a loooong winter can deliver. The air smells of seaweed and woodsmoke: you can almost taste the oxygen. Then, as we leave Robin Hood Bay's rows of Victorian guest houses behind and the cliff path opens up, it smells of sheep dung mixed with the coconuty scent of bright yellow Gorse.

Above our heads swallows loop and dive, their cries punctuated every so often by the whoosh of blackheaded gulls careering through. Beneath the frantic bird calls, the thunder of waves crashing onto the steep wall of North Sea cliffs.

All around is evidence of their ferocity: in some places a small diversion on the path; elsewhere, a raw edge as though someone has taken a giant shovel to the cliffs and gouged out the earth. The coast path is in retreat.

At the top of Robin Hood's Bay a plaque tells a hair-raising story of how unforgiving this landscape can be. Here's what it says:

On the 18th January 1881 the brig 'Visitor' ran ashore in Robin Hood's Bay. No local boat could be launched on account of the vioence of the storm, so the Whitby lifeboat was brought overland past this point – a distance of 6 miles through snowdrifts 7 feet deep on a road rising to 500 feet, with 200 men clearing the way ahead and 18 horses heaving at the tow lines, whilst men worked uphill towards them from the Bay. The lifeboat was launched two hours after leaving Whitby and at the second attempt the crew of the Visitor were saved.

So that future generations may remember the bravery of the Coxswain Henry Freeman and the lifeboatmen, and the dogged determination of the people of Whitby, Hawsker and Robin Hood's Bay, who overcame such difficulties, this memorial was erected in 1981.

I suspect Barry Pincer can trace his roots back to a lifeboatman living in Whitby at the end of the 19th century. As for us, in the two hours it took those 200 men to haul a lifeboat six miles in storm conditions up hill and through snow, Shushie and I have merely reached the caravan park at Hawsker, from where Whitby is still a distant view.

A small diversion

Before Wainwright's love of a long walk made Robin Hood Bay's name synonomous with the Coast to Coast, the town's main claim to fame was probably its connection with the famed outlaw of Sherwood Forest.

Let's be honest, North Yorkshire is a long way from Nottingham, but I suppose even outlaws deserve to take an occasional holiday. According to legend it was the bay's remoteness, naturally hidden from view by virtue of being tucked into a fissure between two cliffs, that sometimes brought Robin Hood north for a reprieve from his life as hunter and hunted. He took the alias of Simon Wise and kept a fleet of fishing boats in which he could put to sea should danger threaten.

What slightly undermines the credibility of this rather lovely image of Robin stripping to his vest and hitting the beach with a tankard of best Yorkshire ale, is nearby Hawsker's rival story – which sees him taking part in the mother of all archery contests.

Far from keeping a low profile it seems Robin and sidekick Little John were visitors to Whitby Abbey, where they were invited to showcase their archery skills. Imagine the fanfare, the crowds flocking up Whitby's narrow streets to the cliff crest which, to this day, is dominated by the Abbey's shell. Their excitement at having the chance to watch two of day's biggest celebrities take each other on from the high Abbey tower.

And if the sight of two legends squaring up on the clifftop wasn't enough to get tongues wagging on every coach and highway from John O'Groats to Land's End, then the sight of their arrows speeding skywards and finally coming to rest *more than 2km* from the Abbey in a farmer's field at Hawsker, would have been.

The Abbot was reputedly so wowed by this display of superhuman ability, that he ordered standing stones to be erected where the arrows landed. (Erected being a rather suitable word for two stones that, from a distance, bear more than a passing resemblance to stone willies – and do note that if the stones are to be believed, Little John surpassed his master by a metre or so.)

None of which storytelling gets us any further along on this Coast to Coast; indeed a visit to the stone willies involves a detour of half a mile or so from the caravan park at Hawsker where Shushie and I are ending day one – a measly four miles from the start.

I told you it was about the journey.

Fast forward to Rosedale

There's much to be said in favour of doing as we've done and taking your time over the Coast to Coast: a weekend here or there, with plenty of time in between to savour what you've seen and to anticipate the next leg.

However, it would be dishonest of me not to share the single biggest drawback of a stutter rather than a sprint from North to Irish Sea.

Logistically, it is a total nightmare.

For those who do the walk in a single gulp there are several services happy to help with routes, accommodation, and – best of all –willing to lug your backpack ahead of you. All you need do is turn up and put one foot in front of the other.

My diaries record the tortuous arrangements we made for the first crossings, involving everything from calling in favours from friends, to taxi rides and crack of dawn trains, through to having two cars in separate Lakeland valleys. Britian is not configured, either naturally or in its infrastructure, for east-west journeying.

Suffice to say that after hours poring over maps the best plan I can come up with is to find accommodation in Rosedale Abbey where we'll be able to leave Shushie's car and cab it back to Hawsker early on day two. Two days' fullish walking will then bring us back to Rosedale, without taking too many liberties with Wainwright's route.

Do Not Try This At Home… by which I mean I am certain you can find a better way than forking out £30 to carry you and your rucksack 20 miles in order to walk those same 20 miles. Wainwright would be turning in his grave.

On the other hand, this back to front scheme does give us the chance to discover a gem of a guest house, Sevenford House, conveniently close to the winner of Yorkshire's Favourite Pub of 2012: the White Horse Farm Inn.

I know you're reading this because you want to hear about the walk but for Shushie and I the good, bad, ugly, and the bloody brilliant bed and breakfasts – not to mention the pubs – are every bit as much a part of the experience. Carry your tent on your back and camp out on the moor if you must; I'm sure it's wonderful waking to the sound of grouse and wind rustling the dry heather.

But even when we first met the Coast to Coast at the fine age of 40, on the threshold of the best years of our lives, Shushie and I preferred Egyptian cotton and hot chips. Now that we are moving inexorably in the direction of 60, a hot bath, soft pillow, lovely hosts, and a full plate of English breakfast, is an absolute necessity.

We've only walked a few miles on this, our first day, but the lovely Linda, who runs Sevenford with husband Ian, has a roaring log fire, pot of Yorkshire tea and plate of biscuits waiting for us in a lounge filled with comfy chairs, bookcases crammed to double thickness, and a view over fields where lambs nibble grass as sumptuous as a perfectly kept lawn.

Stopping in our tracks to watch the light deepen, taste the sharpness of the tea, and watch young rabbits running in circles beside the beck, is the perfect antidote to the full-on, too-busy-to-breathe, lives we've left behind.

Chapter 2: A lot older, a little wiser

The radio has a good feature on pilgrimages this morning, which ends with one of those truisms that slip so easily off the tongue we take its truth for granted: a journey should change you and leave you seeing the world a little differently from how you did at the start.

I'm wary of talking about Our Journey, given the way the term has been hijacked by everyone from tearful reality show contestants to the corporates wanting to flog their wares by taking us on a so-called 'customer journey'.

Let's just say that a lot has changed in the 16 years since Shushie and I first began walking the Coast to Coast – hairstyles included – and we both recognise how many of those changes are due to the space, perspective and reality checking our walking weekends offer.

We've also learned a lot (and NOT learned some things despite the pain of the repeated lessons.) So in the White Horse Farm Inn on that first night we decide to capture them in my notebook.

In case you're planning a walk, a relationship, or on getting older sometime, here they are:

1.   *Respect the hills*: frankly, we're lucky to still be here. I'm inclined to blame dad, who, in an uncharacteristically mad moment back in the early 60s, marched us up Helvellyn via Striding Edge wearing only tee shirts and plimsolls (remember them?). It made us far too casual about stuff like weather reports, correct kit and map-reading skills. More of which anon…

2.   *Always cut your toenails before going walking:* ok, it's not quite in the same life-or-death category as respecting Mother Nature, but NOT cutting your toenails before heading out over hill and dale is a mistake you only make once. Imagine, if you will, someone with ten hammers, trying with every step you take to reinsert your toenails back into the cuticles. That, my friends, is what it feels like to walk down a 1 in 3 gradient in leather boots with unkempt toenails.

3.   *The obvious path is not always the right one:* another rather earnest (sorry) walking/life analogy, but even if you're only interested in walking tips, you need to know this. Just because one path is as wide as a motorway and there are people bombing up and down it, it doesn't mean this is the path you need to take. Sometimes, your path is the mean little track disappearing into the heather where it promptly vanishes. A map helps. And so does a reading of Scott Peck's *The Road Less Travelled*.

4.   *Relationships are not like Hollywood movies:* it's probably just us: you already knew that didn't you? But 16 years, several broken hearts, one divorce and a separation later, we're agreed that if you accept it's not Hollywood it sometimes makes more sense to work at the relationship you're in than go looking again for love's new dream.

5.   *None of us is getting any younger:* I don't mean that in a depressing one foot in the grave sort of way, but rather as a call to arms. One of the reasons we're on this walk is because we need a break from the daily challenges of being carers. And if it wasn't mum – whose own happy, fulfilled and *healthy* life was derailed by a stroke – making us hesitate, it would be something else. The lives most of us have constructed mean there are usually many more reasons

not to do something than to pull on the rucksack and say 'sod it, if not now, when?

6.   ***Talking of which, do more of what makes you happy:*** that's it. You already know what makes us happy. What about you?

7. If you're out walking, and it's on the menu, always order homemade pie: seriously: the steak and stilton pie at the White Horse Farm Inn is the best we've ever tasted – melt in the mouth memorable. Just as every other homemade pie we've ever tucked into at the end of a full day of fresh air, amazing scenery, and energetic walking, has been the best. pies = happiness.

Who ate all the pies? Er..um. That may have been us.

Chapter 3: Falling at the Foss, Hawsker-Egton Bridge

Steak pie was last night. Today's leg – day two of our walk – begins with an early morning taxi ride back to Hawsker to pick up where we left off. Pete, the cabbie, takes it all in his stride, as if it is the most normal thing in the world to be collecting two women claiming to be walkers in order to drive them *out of* the North Yorks Moors national park.

But then Pete lives in Whitby which is under siege this particular weekend from legions of Goths. Compared to this I guess our behaviour scarcely registers on the scale of eccentricity.

(For the curious, Whitby is where Bram Stoker wrote *Dracula*, inspired by the omnipresent shell of Whitby Abbey – yes, the same Abbey that also boasts the Robin Hood connection. And the same Abbey, that as any Coast to Coaster will tell you, remains visible en route for a disconcerting number of days, causing you to wonder whether you have actually travelled any distance at all.)

Forty minutes later we're off down Back Lane, heading towards the edge of the national park, past pretty homes with immaculate gardens, and, at the very edge of Hawsker, the neighbour from hell. Every place has one: the guy who thinks the verges and pavements are simply an extension of his overflowing garage. Approach Hawsker from the moors and the first thing you'll see is a timber yard's worth of wood offcuts piled against the hedgerow and a line of abandoned cars. On the other side of the road, builder's rubble has all but hidden the tiny beck beneath.

Earlier, we'd been flicking through *A Coast to Coast Walk*, relishing one of Wainwright's occasional rants, on this occasion directed at those "careless about the country code, inconsiderate of others, rebels against conventions and customs and decent behaviour and a general nuisance." He calls them Nogs.

We have, it seems, stumbled on the Nog of all Nogs; the ultimate Noggin. The Nogster.

Winding us up

From Back Lane it is a mile or so to reach the Graystone Hills, a slow uphill climb, which gives us our first taste of walking into the prevailing wind Wainwright warns of. At 40 mph – according to that morning's forecast – it feels like someone has a hand on your chest and would prefer you to stay precisely where you are.

I'm going to blame the distractions of wind pressure, hair blown wildly in our eyes, map buffeted from side to side, for the fact that less than an hour into the day we go wrong. Remember what I was saying about being wary of wide paths? When do any of us ever listen to our own advice?

On the one hand, heading in a straight line ahead of us is a clear wide track across the moor. On the other hand, well, nothing really; an indeterminate gap in last season's brown heather that might or might not lead somewhere.

We take the clear track, of course, and fight the wind all the way to the road where we are supposed to be looking for a ladder stile. Instead of which we spot a road sign making it abundantly clear we have completed the third side of a triangle and will now need to fight the wind along the other two sides in order to recover the route.

On a good weather day detours of a mile or so are no hardship. We are high up on the moor, watching the birds preoccupied with courtship rituals, breathing air that tastes of earth, enjoying the shining line of blue sea on the horizon.

Yet on this spring Sunday cars are racing by, presumably desperate to beat their neighbours to the nearest car boot sale, the wind is resisting our every step, and occasional splashes of roadside primrose and cowslip are dwarfed by the foam innards of a sofa, bottles filled with wee, and bits of car wheel and bumpers, abandoned by the Nogs.

Followers not leaders

It is a different story once we rejoin the 'official' route. (Note, Wainwright himself would dissemble here. In the same postscript to his book in which he rails against Nogs, Wainwright also tries to repair the damage caused by the huge popularity of his walk. Insisting that all he is offering is 'an example of what might be done without any opening speeches and fanfares'. He claims *'I would feel I had succeeded better in arousing interest for the planning of private long-distance walks if the book induced some readers to follow instead their own star and find their own rainbow's end'*.An estimated 70,000 plus walkers a year – and growing – are proof that most of us prefer following to trailblazing.)

Indeed, as we head over the ladder stile onto Sneaton Low Moor we encounter the first unmistakeable Coast to Coasters coming dutifully from west to east, the smell of the North Sea already in their lungs – and only the faintest hint of wetness on their boots, good news given that the last time we'd ventured over the moor, on our way to finishing our second crossing, it was literally under water.

From this point on there is no risk of getting lost. Though the guide books suggests rather vaguely that you need to 'head left' across the moor, 70,000 pairs of boots have left their mark. And even if they hadn't, occasional signposts rise high from the heather to ensure walkers can find their way in the foulest weather. The North Yorks Moors are studded with standing stones which must have provided the same comfort to our ancestors.

We rapidly reach the entrance to New May Beck Farm and are bowling down a farm track when a white Dragoman pulls up alongside. The driver leans out the window, cheeks windburned almost to ochre:

"Yer on the Coast to Coast? First day?"

"No, second," Shushie told him.

"Ah, yer've not got far then." He shakes his head sorrowfully at us.

I mention this only because our interviewer turns out to be the farmer, who must see thousands of walkers traipsing across his land. His friendliness seems uncharacteristic, and I wonder if the appearance of a little sun after the longest, harshest, most miserable winter most of us can remember, is responsible.

Dropping down into beautiful May Beck with its picnic benches and nuthatches, swathes of daffodils and sun dapples on the surface of the water, reminds me of the scene in Narnia where winter finally ends and the snow melts and everything comes to joyful, vibrant life. For now, we have left the wind behind, the bleak moorland scenery has morphed into mossbanks and the magical tree shapes of a fairy glade. Oh, it is good to be alive, and away and noticing it all.

Mind the gap

There's noticing and noticing of course. For a while we meander alongside the beck, enjoying its sound as it trickles over rocks, spilling out into wide pools, then narrowing again to nudge a way around tree roots en route to the dramatic Falling Foss waterfall.

We're heading there too, drawn by the low thrum of tumbling water ahead, sure of the path as we've visited this lovely woodland twice before.

Silly mistake, as it turns out.

Shushie announces that we need to cross some stepping stones and leads us purposefully down to a place where the beck has broadened out.

"Are you sure? This doesn't seem quite right," I offer half-heartedly. It's not that I have a better suggestion. Simply that on a trail used by so many Wainwright acolytes these so-called stepping stones seem rather inadequate.

"I'm sure we have to cross. I'll go ahead and check."

The next 30 seconds happen in slow motion.

Shushie is halfway across when one foot slips off the wet rocks. Her leg follows her foot off the stone and down a ledge into the pool of water below. Off balance now, Shushie scrabbles for a foothold, handhold, any kind of hold.

There is none to be had. Everything is wet and slick and the weight of her pack follows the momentum of her sliding leg so that the rest of her has no choice but to follow, down the ledge, into the water, until she is half lying on her back, fully clothed, up to her chest in the beck.

And here I have a confession. I am not proud of it but it is an interesting reflection, I think, on how much of our lives we now expect to live out on Facebook or YouTube or Twitter or – heaven help me for I have sinned many times over by laughing myself helpless at fainting bridegrooms, collapsing paddling pools and *people falling off logs and boats into rivers – You've Been Framed.*

As Shushie flounders and swears and tries to prevent the rest of her, including camera, phone and head going under, I waver between getting out my own camera to film her and racing over to help. Oh, shame!

Of course it's too late to offer much in the way of help. The damage is done and even though, in the end, my camera phone stays in my pocket, I can do little more than follow her across the river, fussing ineffectually.

"Shittity, shittity, shit shit," Shushie says, rather mildly I think,

22

considering the water is gushing from her pockets and trouser legs like Boxing Day Sale shoppers through the door of Selfridges. My own thoughts are already in this-is-a-disaster mode. We are four miles into a 14 mile day, of which the biggest chunk will involve moorland, 40 mph winds, and therefore wind-chill. There is no way on earth Shushie can go on.

"What are we going to do?"

"I need to get out of these wet clothes. I've got another pair of trousers and some knickers in the rucksack."

"What, change here?"

"Yes."

She is as businesslike and focused as I am faffy and useless, fiddling to get my jacket off so I can offer some shield for her modesty as if we were on Brighton Beach.

By the time I find somewhere halfway dry to place her rucksack and fiddle in it for the spare set of clothes Shushie is naked from the waist down and, frankly, couldn't care less if there is anyone around to enjoy the flash of sopping skin. She flicks pointlessly at her legs with a small pink bandana, trying to soak up the worst of it.

"What about your boots. You can't walk the rest of the day in sodden boots. Why don't you change into the shoes you've brought for tonight?"

"I would if they were trainers but they're pumps. No way can I walk in them. I'll have to stay in these."

"Well at least put on some dry socks."

For the first and only time during the whole episode Shushie's matter of factness falters. "Er, WHY?"

And that, friends, is another secret of successful walking. Choose the right companion; someone who will pick themselves up, put on dry knickers, and plug on. Or, in Shushie's case, squelch on.

For those of you following in our footsteps east to west, you may like to know that, around a bend in the beck, 50 metres further on from the 'stepping stones', there's a big fat bridge to take you safely across.

The Great Escape: Littlebeck-Egton Bridge

Falling Foss waterfall and its tearoom are only one of the attractions bringing weekenders into Littlebeck Wood. Half a mile further along the mossy track which follows the beck you come across the hideout of another character who apparently preferred the company of nature and his own solitary footsteps, to crowds – an 18th century Wainwright if you will.

The Hermitage is a large dank cave hewn out of a single limestone rock, its creator's initials GC – for George Chubb – etched so deep above the doorway they are as clear now as they must have been when he first carved the 18th century equivalent of 'get orf my land' in 1790.

More than one of the Coast to Coast guide books suggests the Hermitage is a useful spot to take shelter. But to us there's something vaguely unpleasant about it: the unsocial Mr Chubb's vibe perhaps, still trapped in the graffitied walls and, skunk-like, repelling those who dare to approach his hideaway even two centuries on.

We head, instead, out of the woods and into the hamlet of Littlebeck, which is as pretty and welcoming as the Hermitage is dour – a place that got even Wainwright's juices flowing, for in a rare flourish he describes it as *'a miniature Arcadia embowered in trees, a glimpse of heaven for nerve-frayed town-dwellers'*.

Cottage gardens bursting with spring colour…tick. Perfectly kept houses sheltered in a peaceful valley between coast and moors…tick.

A shallow ford to delight children and anyone driving a 4 x 4…tick. Benches on every bend, so that nerve-frayed town-dwellers (Shushie and I) can sit and eat sandwiches in a pleasantly ambivalent state of peace and envy…another tick.

Escape to the country

Twice before as we walked from Coast to Coast Littlebeck provoked the same thoughts of escape in us: of doing a George Chubb and leaving our lives behind to go to ground in a tiny, hidden Yorkshire hamlet.

To be honest Littlebeck isn't the only place Shushie and I have had the escape conversation. It may just possibly have come up pretty much every time we walked.

The truth is that for much of the time we've been walking in Wainwright's footsteps I've experienced life at home as such a struggle that even a dog kennel in Littlebeck seemed preferable to returning to Milton Keynes at the end of a weekend.

I'm not a fan of 70s sitcoms but one scene that seems to have branded itself on my consciousness is the moment in *The Rise and Fall of Reggie Perrin* where Reggie stands on a beach contemplating faking his own death in order to escape from a monotonous job, difficult relationships and a midlife crisis.

Oops, another big tick.

Of course, one of the things those years of overwhelm finally taught me was that old truism: that *wherever you go, there you are*. During our first Coast to Coast walk we came across plenty of townies who'd headed north to live the second half of their lives in their personal Arcadia: the Moors, the Dales, the Lakes.

Those who were still there by the time we returned (and there were only a few) were the ones who weren't running away from anything;

they just wanted to do what they did with added view.

They wanted more, not less.

I'd also learned – eventually - that the best, and often the only way to 'escape' was by changing what went on inside my own head.

During the early walking years the urge to run for the hills was more than anything a desire to silence my own mental soundtrack of stress, dissatisfaction and doubt. That's a whole other story, of course, but recognising it did help me come closer to understanding George Chubb ... and his successor, the famously solitary Alfred Wainwright.

Wind and wuthering

Talking of whom, it is time to leave Arcadia and rejoin Wainwright's Coast to Coast, heading back out onto the moor, before our muscles that, to be honest, have not been much tested for the last, err, seven years, have a chance to atrophy. That's what happens when you're not fit and you take too long over your Marks and Spencer salad – especially when an unscheduled dip in the beck has added to the chill factor.

And also, when you have been this way before and know that to leave Littlebeck involves a long, arduous climb, **up** a twisting country lane to cross the road and then **up** an almost perpendicular farm track to cross another road leading out – you've guessed it –**up** again onto the moortop.

But it is worth the breathless slog up onto the roof of this part of the world. Sleights Moor may be wild and the wind may whip your words away before they can be spoken, but it offers the most fantastic panoramas, back to the sea and, 180 degrees around, out over the lush Esk valley, whose gentle slopes are as fresh as lime peel.

We have no choice but to take our time climbing to the plateau of the moor – but once there the lowering clouds assembling over

Grosmont and Egton Bridge – our goals – urge us to push ourselves forward. The steady slap of our footsteps on the high moor road rapidly turns into a route march.

From Sleights the Coast to Coast follows the road down into Grosmont, past rows of terraced homes whose blackened bricks seem more suited to the backstreets of a northern town during the industrial revolution than to a remote moorland village.

The culprit, it turns out, is the steam railway line: the work of a small group of railway geeks who decided that their great escape would be into the past, keeping alive a section of the old Pickering to Whitby line which was once such a vital part of the ironworking industry in this part of Yorkshire.

Blast from the past

This year they are celebrating the 40th anniversary of the reopening of the North Yorkshire Moors Railway – coincidentally the same number of years since Wainwright's *A Coast to Coast Walk* first appeared.

Our arrival in Grosmont coincides with that of a train coupled to Pullman carriages. It's packed with people who've paid premium prices to enjoy a journey with cupcakes, champagne and starched waiters rather than mobile phone ringtones.

Alongside, the scheduled steam train from Whitby pulls in, its passengers, surreally, including a contingent of Goths, as black and polished as the boots of the station volunteers.

One of the loveliest things about the North Yorks Railway is how wholehearted it all is. Scarcely a detail has been missed, from the colour-coded lamps on the level crossing gates to the waiting room, which might be straight from the set of *Brief Encounter*.

We stand on the platform for a moment, allowing the self-important blast of whistles and bursts of steam to take us back a century. But even with the temptations of cupcakes, I would not swap walking for rail travel on this day. The last mile of this leg takes us onto an old toll road, now no more than a farm track, beside the shining Esk, flanked by fields whose green is dotted with the red and gold of grazing pheasant. The clouds have moved on. The track is flat and fast.

It is all as picture-perfect as the moors have been ancient and wild: Beatrix Potter rather than Emily Bronte – even down to the old stone pigsty we pass, where Pigling Bland might once have lived.

Egton Bridge seems similarly perfect, a sort of Littlebeck Extra, with a wider river and longer gardens and a great deal more in the way of hospitality. It also has its own saint and martyr, one Nicholas Postgate whose birth in Egton Bridge in 1596 is commemorated at St Hedda's Catholic Church in the village.

Secrets

I suppose it's a little like our attraction to the steam railway: from the comfort and distance of the 21st century it's easy to romanticise the life of the North Yorkshire Moors and imagine our ancestors living in tune with the seasons and scenery, dependent on family and neighbours, content with the small things in life and strangers to stress (and ringtones).

Far from being a rural idyll though, 17th century Egton Bridge was a village of secrets and seige, fiercely – but secretively - Catholic while the rest of the UK went through Reformation.

At the age of 25 Postgate slipped away to France to train as a priest, then returned to the moors to live and share his faith, disguised as a gardener.

Travelling around the area incognito, he spent more than five decades ministering to the sick, giving communion and saying mass, before he was trapped conducting a baptism at the implausibly-named Ugglebarnby.

The fact that when Postgate was caught ministering to closet Catholics at the age of 82, the law still chose to hang, draw and quarter 'the martyr of the moors', demonstrates just what brutal and fearful times those were – a world away from the tourists meandering down moorland roads and stopping for a cold beer and ploughmans at The Horseshoe.

We are heading to the Horseshoe later, but first we have an appointment with our favourite of all guest houses on any Coast to Coast journey we've made: Broom House.

And that's where I'll leave you in this chapter, picturing us opening the door on a room under the eaves that looks out over pasture and river to the high moor; from where we can hear the Esk gently flowing over boulders, while fat pillows, huge fluffy bath towels, hot tea and homemade oat biscuits await.

That's the other thing about escape: sometimes it's just a moment.

Chapter 4: The Great British B&B: good, bad and downright ugly

As the number of visitors walking Wainwright's route have increased, so has the number of guest houses, luggage carriers, and even Coast to Coast fish and chip shops, to service them.

We've sampled a fair few: most perfectly adequate, if not particularly memorable. But then bear in mind much of our early walking took place in pre-Trip Advisor days, when we had no means of finding out in advance that the only door into or out of *our* bedroom was through the other guest's bedroom (Glenridding), or that guests might need to have everything from teamaking equipment to light switches helpfully identified with blue plastic labels (Ennerdale Bridge).

And had Trip Advisor been around in the late 1990s think what we'd have missed...

The *bad*, certainly, which came at the end of a cold January day when we'd slogged along 20 miles of tarmac and mud. As a treat Shushie decided we'd forgo our usual humble b&b and booked us a little luxury at Catterick's main hotel, The Bridge House Hotel.

Hmm, Catterick. The sort of place people go for a luxury break. Not.

Think 1960s Blackpool and you'll have the room decor down to a tee. And then think opposite the racecourse, paper thin walls, and two stable staff going for it like Grand National runners in the double bed a few inches from our heads. Think of the noisiest sex and the crudest swear words you can imagine (or don't, if that's already too much information). I think Shushie and I may have left that hotel around 8am the following day, desperate not to have to eyeball our noisy neighbours over the breakfast table.

And yes, I do blame the hotel. Why would any hotel, that has 20 rooms and only four guests staying the night, put them in adjacent rooms?

Barefaced cheek

And then there was the *truly ugly*, not a million miles away as it happens, though the scenery in Reeth, on the edge of the Yorkshire Dales, has more going for it than Catterick.

We followed our noses to this particular b&b, which overlooked Reeth's large village green. There's nothing wrong with the smell of cooking garlic. It just came as a bit of a surprise to be able to smell it from half a mile away.

The second surprise was our little bedroom which had been advertised as en suite. An estate agent would call it bijou. I call it plain freaky to stick a glass shower cabinet at the end of a double bed so that your roommate is on full technicolour display as they perform their ablutions.

It was downhill from there. A knock on the door – fortunately at a time when neither of us was in the shower - because the landlady needed to know what time we wanted breakfast. We were booked onto the Packhorse – the transport and luggage service for Coast to Coasters - for a lift to our starting point and had to fit around its timetable which meant a 7.30 am start from the village green.

Cue a frightening meltdown from our hostess. She ought to have been given more notice that we needed an early breakfast. It was quite impossible.

Her tone was as rude as that dammed shower cabinet.

Well perhaps you could leave out a loaf , toaster and the kettle? It's no problem, we'll get our own, we tentatively suggested, never liking to cause trouble.

Another rant. Guests were apparently prohibited from using any electrical equipment.

Bread and jam then? No, the bread would be stale (apparently they don't have cling film in Reeth). Why ever hadn't we warned her? Other guests *booked* their early breakfast.

This was the point at which I decided I didn't want to spend another moment in garlic hell and began to say as much to my sister.

We don't always call her Shushie. Sometimes she's Shush.

Imagine our already apoplectic landlady when I turned to my sister and said loudly 'Shush....'

I didn't get to say anything else. We only got to listen as the glass walls of the shower cabinet rattled to her shrieks and, downstairs in the restaurant the hum of conversation and cutlery suddenly transformed to horrified silence.

I'd tell you the name of the place but by the time we returned on our west to east walk it had gone out of business.

Can't imagine why.

Simply the best

So finally, to the *good*, like Sevenford House, our previous night's heaven on earth, and Broom House in Egton Bridge, which we first encountered in its very first season under the ownership of David and Maria White. Exiles from the city, they'd spent months converting an old farmhouse into the sort of place any walker fantasises about, from the bliss of deep baths, to friendly customer service in the face of even the muddiest boots.

You know you've found somewhere special when your hosts are willing to check maps and weather reports for you, provide torches for after-dark walks to the local, offer packed lunches and claim to remember you each time you return.

They even ask if we want an early breakfast...

Chapter 5: Sticks and stones: Egton Bridge-Rosedale Abbey

These days canny walkers carry sticks. They may make you look like a geriatric but they really do make a difference to the effort you have to put into moving forward. Don't ask me how: I'm sure scientists can explain it, but for me it still feels like magic.

Plus there's a nice continuity to the clipped clicking sound walking sticks make on stone. It's a reminder that once upon a time these same routes echoed to the sound of horseshoes and the nails in leather boots, as the people of the moors trod them for livelihood rather than leisure.

Our day begins, for example, with acrossing of the Esk via two causeways of stout stepping stones, their surfaces scooped by tens of thousands of feet over many centuries seeking a shortcut out of Egton Bridge.

The stones sit high out of the water, which means they are bone dry and Shushie is in no danger of sliding off them this time. Still, she moves tentatively, like a tightrope walker with vertigo and no safety net.

For a short spell the Coast to Coast route follows a quiet moors lane, before peeling off into Arncliffe Woods where we join an ancient pannier route, wide enough for horses – and those too poor to own animals – carrying heavy baskets laden with goods to sell, or provisions bought from the market.

Instead of the creaking of leather harnesses and wicker our soundtrack is birdsong – and an exasperated local trying to call her

Rescue dog, Benji, to heel as he bounces towards us, all shaggy hair and flapping ears.

The woods are straight from *A Midsummer Night's Dream*, lush and full of hidden places. It's easy to imagine fairies and sprites watching from dark gaps in the tangled tree roots or asleep in the blankets of moss covering the ground.

There are brown pools among the roots, and cowslips, forget me nots and violets: tiny little jewels of colour. And we might have slipped into the pages of a storybook ourselves, except that a side path peels off to a ledge from where we can see an ugly steel bridge, carrying the railway over the Esk far below.

Hearts and stone

As we approach Glaisdale the woodland path gives way to wide limestone paving slabs, which must have made descent and ascent easier for those laden travellers during wet and icy winter months. Their surfaces are smooth from generations of travellers, as we drop steeply down to river level, rejoining the Esk at Beggars Bridge.

It's always nice to receive flowers and chocolates from the man/woman in your life, but be honest, don't you sometimes yearn for the big gesture? A bridge, say?

Yep. Beggar's Bridge, built from local stone in 1619, is said to be the work of one Tom Ferris who fell in love with Agnes, the daughter of a wealthy farmer. Our boy Tom faced two main obstacles: firstly, Agnes lived on the opposite side of the Esk, which (this being the UK) was often in full, impassable flood. Secondly, and rather less romantically, Agnes' father disapproved of her feelings for a local lad with no prospects.

Heartbroken, Tom ran off to fight the Spanish Armada and discovered it's an ill wind… For with war came the opportunity to loot Spanish galleons and he was eventually able to return to

Yorkshire and win around both father and daughter – one with his new money; the other with this rather unique love token – a bridge over the river, so that other lovers would no longer be separated by the vagaries of the weather.

Agnes may not have been able to wear it around her neck, but she was clearly impressed for, reader, she married him.

The long and winding road

Glaisdale itself sprawls across the valley, a strange mix of attractive country seats and functional rows of houses that date, perhaps, from the 19th century when the hills around the village were mined for the iron that kept Middlesborough's furnaces supplied.

You'd never think that now. We see scarcely a soul as we wind our way uphill past closed-up homes along one side of the valley and then around a sharp bend and up again by more vacant windows to Glaisdale's only two shops.

One is a tiny general store, the other an equally compact butcher's whose window display of extravagant meat cuts and mince mountains looks like nothing I have ever seen in a supermarket.

We are probably a disappointment to the butcher, Shushie and I, passing over the slabs of pork and beef in favour of a couple of individual quiches which will serve as lunch.

"Quiche?" he laughs at our southerness. "Thar's just a posh name fer eggnbeckon pie."

It's not just us who don't pass muster either. We tell him we're doing the Coast to Coast a weekend at a time. He nods approvingly. "Sum folk are mad, doin' it in two or three weeks. Yer've got to tek your time and enjoy it or what's point?"

Fingertips

Today we are sure we know the point. It's so that you don't have to start thinking, almost as soon as you start, about the fact that it will soon be over and you'll be heading back home.

Earlier that day, lying in bed watching the sunlight moving across the covers each time the breeze lifted the window blinds, I caught the smell of mum's house: cat food and staleness. It was only for a moment, but it was enough to remind me that at the end of this day there will be no soft, strange bed and lazy talk but a long drive back home to our responsibilities.

The previous two days have been possibly the first time in the three and a half years since mum got ill that we have not spent most of our together time discussing the practicalities of our care roles: who will do what when and what else we need to organise and plan for and think about and prepare.

The forward planning and logistics involved in even these three short days away was boggling.

Of course we're not the first, and we certainly won't be the last carers to sometimes feel we are hanging on by our fingertips. But the thing about life throwing you a curve ball is that it can often seem that the only way to keep it up in the air along with all the others is by switching modes to automatic. Get up, get on.

Which gets you through days dominated by 'to do' lists more or less intact. But is also removes you from the real raw experience of living your life.

I don't have any answers when Shushie says it may have been back in 2009 that she was last aware of living in the moment; consciously being in her own life. That's another reason these weekends matter.

Timeless

So in the spirit of being in the moment, let me share with you the joy of once again leaving buildings behind and striding out onto Glaisdale Moor following the Rigg – which, oddly, I have learned from a website on baby names (seriously, would you?) means ridge.

Glaisdale Rigg cuts wide and straight past grouse butts and a dark pond full of tadpoles to the horizon where we join the road for a brief spell before peeling off towards Danby High Moor and its long, protective sweep around the wonderfully named Great Fryup Dale.

This is the Yorkshire Moors at their most dramatic, created on a scale that explains exactly why those who had to cross them erected standing stones and causeways, for comfort as much as convenience.

Below us in the dale, a patchwork of green fields and stone barns and a scattering of farms and cottages. And up above, where we stop and perch with our egg and bacon pies, nothing surviving the wildness of the winds above knee height. In every direction, an expanse of brown bracken and dormant heather. An indifferent landscape, virtually unchanged since the days of the panniers.

The last stage of this leg for us is to leave the official Coast to Coast and join the George Gap Causeway back to the moors road and from there to Rosedale Abbey and Shushie's car.

Apparently this paved causeway once ran from Rosedale to Staithes on the North Sea coast but the ever-practical Yorkshire folk found a better use for the stones in their homes and farm buildings. Which does mean that from time to time our boots sink down into bog.

But you don't need to know about this because by now we are thoroughly off piste – and though Wainwright would probably approve of our taking liberties with his route ('vary it to suit yourself') we're purists at heart and the three miles back to Rosedale don't really count.

Except in so far as they can be used to justify the fresh cream scones we polish off at an empty tearoom in Rosedale Abbey before heading for home.

We are less than an hour into the four and a half hour journey when we get the call from Age UK's alarm centre. Mum has had a fall at home and hit her head and can we get there right away to let the paramedics in?

The law of sod.

And very definitely a dropped ball.

Chapter 6: Beware the Moor, Rosedale – Blakey Ridge

I've already mentioned that the Coast to Coast taught us respect for the mountains. But the moors are no pushover either.

Leaving aside the chances of stumbling out of *The Slaughtered Lamb* straight into the jaws of a Yorkshire werewolf (for those under the age of 40 a reference to *An American Werewolf in London* in which it all starts going horribly wrong for two hapless US students when they get lost on the moors) it seems we are in greater danger from the things Hollywood overlooked.

According to a sign we encounter early on the late spring day we return to pick up where we left the walk, if we're not careful we could die from a) Lyme Disease caused by sheep ticks burrowing into us b) adder bites or c) bog.

The last of these seems the most likely. When we last came this way in 2006, towards the end of our second Coast to Coast crossing, the moors were blanketed under a layer of dense, seeping fog. On either side of a narrow stone path the bog oozed and sucked malignly.

On that occasion we were heading for the famous Lion Inn, a fairly ordinary pub, whose isolated position on a lonely road at the top of the moors has undeservedly earned it the status among walkers of Everest base camp.

We knew we were getting close because through the damp heaviness of fog we picked up the reassuring whiff of woodsmoke. Somewhere out there in the fog others were as disoriented as us for suddenly there came the shrill, urgent sound of a whistle. It sounded three or four times: the signal of walkers trying to find each other in the blankness.

Tentatively we edged forward, unnerved by the alarm. "I'm sure we should be there by now." My voice sounded nervous in the suffocating white-out.

"Yes," Shushie stopped. "I could smell the fire a while ago but it seems to have gone now."

We stood there together, until Shushie thought to turn around. "Is it my imagination or is the fog a different colour there? It's not a building is it?"

Blacker, fuzzy and unclear, but unmistakeably something other than fresh air and moorland. We had walked right past the front door of the pub, its car park, cellars, and half a dozen outbuildings.

Today, couldn't be more different. Almost uniquely for a British bank holiday, there is no sign of fog or drizzle, in fact *the sun is out.* Which means that everyone who owns a set of wheels has decided on a drive out onto the moors for lunch at The Lion.

Nothing as natural as change

Our feelings are decidedly mixed as we realise we'll be sharing this day's walking not only with Coast to Coasters but picnickers in laybys, the whip-your-shirt-off-at-the-first-sign-of sun brigade, and probably more than a few nogs.

On the other hand, this time we can see where we were going – including the Lion on its perch in the far distance; it feels as if we might be able to see the whole of Yorkshire, out across the patchwork of brown-bruised heather, unfurling bracken and spikey grass.

We might even, as we rejoin the official route at Trough House, be able to glimpse the sea, away to the east.

We are on a plateau, on top of the world, breathing in the space and the colours and the smell of grass and sheep and new growth.

And that's why I'm bothering to tell you about our earlier trips, for the sake of those who are wondering why we'd choose to do the same walk a third time, when there is so much else out there, so many other hills and dales and moors to explore.

Here's my answer. Because the natural world is never the same two days in a row. It doesn't only change year to year and season to season but hour by hour. Each time you return it offers new gifts.

Already on this day we have seen and heard for the first time curved-beak curlews swooping over the heather above their nests of new chicks; the scarlet-hooded eyes of grouse observing us watchfully; cotton grass puffs waving in the wind; and above them all, the contrails of planes dissolving away into thin fingers which seem to be beckoning us on.

Change is the way of things – a theme that has been front of mind for Shushie and I since we drove north the previous day, pondering midlife and this sense that in some way our lives also have plateaued. Mum's illness and need for us has changed everything and has made many of the changes we might choose for ourselves impossible.

For two people whose lives have almost never stopped moving, reconfiguring around circumstance, need and desire, it feels as if we've been shunted into the sidings, watching as the rest of the world passes by.

"We don't sit well with marking time," is how Shushie describes it.

And yet here, all around us on this perfect spring day, is the lesson. That even when you think you're stuck, beneath the surface everything is shifting. Even the 'us' looking out on all this beauty and natural ebb and flow.

I know there'll come a time when we look back on these years and realise how far we really did travel.

In the meantime, it's best foot forward, on towards the Lion.

Chapter 7: Rolling with the stones, Blakey Ridge – Clay Bank Top

You've got to feel a little sorry for 'Fat Betty'.

Squat, stolid, naked from the waist down, this standing stone is visible for miles. But while history has celebrated her nearest neighbour – the thrusting 'Young Ralph' cross – by making him the symbol of the North York Moors National Park, poor old Betty is noted merely for her girth.

No-one seems to know precisely how this stone – referred to on maps as White Cross – got her nickname. One school of thought says she may be named for a Rosedale Abbey nun called Elizabeth, who, like all the sisters, wore an off-white habit made from undyed sheep's wool – and ate all the pies the convent kitchen could turn out.

Which story may explain why, when Shushie and I reach Fat Betty on the Rosedale to Blakey Ridge road, we find an odd selection of edible offerings left by grateful walkers: half a cheese salad sandwich wrapped in cling film, one Rowntrees fruit pastille, a corner of Kendal mint cake and a Titan chocolate bar. It would explain why the poor old girl hasn't managed to lose weight in five centuries.

Strangers in the heather

We're heading towards Fat Betty when we encounter the most unlikely couple of hikers, dressed for the golf club rather than the wilderness. He's dressed in sharp slacks beneath a camel waistcoat . His shoes, of toffee-coloured leather, are polished to the gloss of a walnut cabinet.

Two hundred metres further is a woman inching forward with the help of two wooden sticks.

Shushie and I are down to tee-shirts already but she's wearing woollens and a pleated skirt and a thick jacket. Only her legs reveal less-than-perfect grooming for they're bare and a little mottled. The flesh of her feet bulges over the sides of leather slip-ons.

"Good morning. Lovely day isn't it?" she greets us in stockbroker tones.

"Gorgeous. Is that your husband up ahead?"

"Yes," her bright smile falters. "I can't keep up with him at all. It's hard for me to walk you see. I've had four knee operations now, and then one of them knocked my back out so they had to operate on that too.

"You'd never guess I used to walk miles on the golf course; four times a week sometimes," the smile has gone altogether now. "Loved it. I never thought this would happen to me, but I suppose I'm 80 now. That's how it goes. Oh well…"

Shushie sympathises and talks a bit about mum and the randomness of ill health happening to people who seem so energetic and have looked after themselves all their lives. It reminds me of when we were talking on the journey up about our own midlife with all its possibilities and challenges, her words: "I am confronted on a daily basis with what the ageing process can do to a vigorous woman." Which ought to be an incentive to live life now, but, on some days, feels more like fear.

I feel the same ambivalence at the sight of this woman. On the one hand, admiration for her dogged determination to get out and taste the air, however much it costs her to do so on two awkward sticks. And on the other hand, fear for her, that somehow it's all too raw a reminder of what she can no longer do.

"I know I ought to walk more. The doctors tell me I should, but they don't realise it's not easy. And the weather's been so awful…

"Oh well," she says for the second time, and it is one of the most bitter sweet 'oh wells' I have ever heard.

We say our goodbyes and possibly we walk on a little slower, conscious of not allowing our joyful energetic steps to add to her burden.

Moors and miners

The Lion Inn today may be a favourite among weekend trippers but its' history is darker.

Like everything in this part of the moor, from the scarred hillsides still visible beneath the heather, to the old railway track we are about to join, the Lion Inn's heyday coincided with the mining of this landscape for iron ore. It was a watering hole for grafters caked in the grime of hard labour rather than townies in search of sun and scampi. (The Lion's own website says that before the miners came the inn may once have been owned and run by monks who went by the brilliant name of the Order of *Crouched* Friars – clearly as cowed by the wind as we have been).

The monks and miners are long departed and any chance of glimpsing their bent ghosts or catching the echo of pickaxes on ironstone is drowned for us by speeding cars and noisy crowds on benches outside the Inn.

So we pass quickly up, past the old burial mound which was once used for cockfighting, to reach the former track of the Rosedale Ironstone Railway, now transformed to a wide footpath for people carrying daypacks and cameras rather than axes.

Remember Betty, and her convent community lower down the valley at Rosedale Abbey? Like the crouching monks earning their keep by brewing and serving ale, the nuns of Rosedale had a lucrative sideline, after Edward III granted them the rights in 1328 to mine iron ore in the dale and far beyond.

I don't imagine the nuns rolled up their habits and set to work themselves; they would have used local labour to bring home the iron that could then be sold to support the Abbey's good works (and keep Betty in pies).

That continued to be the case for centuries – until the advent of the industrial revolution and the ravenous furnaces of Teeside which swallowed up raw resources in a way this country had not known before.

At the height of the mining operation more than five million tons of iron were extracted by hand and transported across some of the most inhospitable landscape imaginable in the space of just 20 years. Imagine the noise and the sweat, the brutality of those times for both labourers and the landscape they worked.

Bouncing along the track in glorious sunshine Shushie and I struggle to imagine. It's remarkable, and also comforting, how seamlessly the moor has crept back over the scars to reclaim the wildness for itself and the creatures that live from it.

Only in places do we see reminders of its historic past: a digger has been through recently, clearing the ditch on one side of the path to prevent flooding. And as water seeps off the moor into the new channel in places it is the red of dried blood: liquid iron. Occasionally old sleepers from the track have been used to shore up the path, sodden and holed as cork as they slowly rot into the ground.

We spot an occasional relic too: a handworked nail that may once have held a miner's tool together, rusted hinges, a long whorled pin, and plenty of shiny nuggets of what could be ironstone.

Lost from Liverpool

The fact that we have time to look for industrial debris is testament to what easy walking this is. There is no doubt about which is the right path, and the number of people coming in groups from the other direction confirms we've hit a Coast to Coast highway.

We know they're us in reverse because each group is carrying a Coast to Coast guidebook – though, remarkably, we don't spot the same book twice. Perhaps new and improved versions of Wainwright's original guide are the industry that has replaced mining...

For those who enjoy such details, we're using a guide by Terry Marsh, solely because he appears to be the only writer with the nouse to realise some people prefer to travel east to west. At the back of his book is a hefty section dedicated to assisting walkers travelling from Robin Hood's Bay to St Bees, with the proviso that 'walkers going against the flow will need to be reasonably good navigators'.

Not us then. Shushie and I have been lost more times than we've used blister plasters (a lot), but that afternoon on the Rosedale Ironstone Railway we're in for a treat – three women who are worse at navigation than us.

We meet them near Bloworth Crossing, the point where the five-mile trek along the railway bed ends, and we leave Farndale to join the Cleveland Way across Urra Moor, via more lonely standing stones. It's clear, even from a distance, that they're looking for a chance to stop and chat with everyone they pass. When they reach us we learn why.

"My feet are killing," says the dark-haired smiley one in a broad Scouse accent. "Don't think we've got any chance of making it to the bed and breakfast tonight."

"Have you come far then?"

"Nah. It's just me. Unfit."

One of her companions jumps in with an explanation. "We've been doing it for 18 months, a weekend at a time. Not enough days at a time to get used to the walking. It's only when we can all get together, and that's hard."

The third woman, who had been looking a little detached, suddenly bursts to life. "COMMITMENTS."

All five of us nod sagely at the dirty word.

"We may not be fit but we're great at getting lost," chips in the dark one again. "Worst time was on Kirsty. Is that what it's called?" she turns to her companions who shrug their own lack of certainty about even this detail. "We went wrong and ended up at Pooley Bridge. Eight miles or something out of the way."

Let me just say here that, first, Kirsty is a girls's name and the place where they went wrong was Kidsty, which is an unforgiving pike sitting atop High Street and connecting the valleys of Ullswater and Haweswater. And second, that Pooley Bridge lies at the very end of Ullswater, eleven miles from the lake head, and several thousand feet below Kidsty. It is also in precisely the opposite direction from the onward route on the Coast to Coast.

They hadn't just taken a minor detour. This was getting lost on an epic, Lakeland-sized scale. And by comparison it makes us look like total professionals.

Pride before a fall

The only ones who don't shout a greeting as they pass us are the cyclists. Most whizz by in a fury of lycra and sunglasses, the set of their jaws proclaiming that wheels have right of way over walking boots.

Especially when we reach Urra Moor which is altogether darker and bleaker than the Rosedale path, but perhaps preferred by the silent cyclists because it has more ups and downs to challenge them.

The most significant of these downs comes at the end of our

day's leg, as the path descends from Urra across a field and down to a busy car park at Clay Bank Top.

Descends being too bland a description for the way the path hurls itself down the gradient, between rocks and slippery shale – explaining why there is a sign at the top warning cyclists to dismount.

We've just begun our plunge when a group of three cyclists scream up behind, their leader officiously demanding that we move out of their way – rather like those people in swimming pools who are doing lengths and assume, as their fingernails gouge into your back, that you will be the one to shift.

Bringing up the rear the third cyclist teeters past, guiding his front wheel straight into a gulley, from which the momentum and angle send the bike in a slow somersault, catapulting the rider over its handlebars and onto his head further down the slope. We hover, wondering whether we ought to go and check up on him or if his mates will notice and come back. But before we can decide anything he's jumped up with fake bravado, dusts himself off and is back on his bike.

"And that's why there's a sign at…" Shushie starts to say to me, before the cyclist's bike wheel slips into a second gulley, and we watch in disbelief as his bike does a second 360 degree spin while he skids and slides most of way down what remains of the hill.

We are not, we've learned this afternoon, the thickest slices in the loaf. Not by a long way.

Chapter 8: Doreen Whitehead, a Coast to Coast legend

We heard about Doreen Whitehead on our first Coast to Coast crossing: her hospitality was legendary among walkers.

So it would be remiss not to tell you about her in an account of our time on the Coast to Coast. The best journeys are, after all, so much more than the miles that are covered. People, events, and the memories we ourselves create transform a flat map into one of those three dimensional cross sections that show all the layers making up the landscape of our lives.

Doreen, it turned out, was a layer all of her own.

It was 2005 and the end of one of our wettest-ever days on the Coast to Coast. We found Doreen in the hallway of Butt House, a stout, slightly old-fashioned bed and breakfast in the Dales village of Keld. She was sitting squarely behind a desk, checking in each group of sodden arrivals and issuing welcome and instructions in a booming Yorkshire accent.

"Ah, dunna worry boout a bit of wet. That's how tis with walkers. Wi've a drying room for yer boots. Mind, summa you walkers are right dim. I allus tell 'em to put stuff on radiator, but do they 'eck?"

"Now, see thy room but come right down; thes a pot a tea, scons and kek in lounge."

I doubt it ever occurred to any of Doreen's guests to argue. It was her house and her way, right down to those warm scones which arrived with an inch of yellow butter already applied – just in case any guest mistakenly thought they might get away with jam alone. Here was someone so conscious of her status as one of the best hosts en route that she would probably rather have turned guests away than fail to have scones and a chocolate cake the size of a small country awaiting their arrival.

Lost and found

And that was merely the appetiser. As we tucked in Doreen, notebook in hand, reeled off the four choices we had for each of three courses at the dinner yet to come. It was all larger than life: the food, Doreen's character, and the vast fund of stories with which she commanded the oval dining table when we and the other guests sat down to work a tentative way through heaving plates of the most brilliantly home-cooked food.

Her first theme was how hard it was to make a living from bed and breakfast, and her deep regret that the following year she'd have to increase the price of an evening meal from £11 to £12. It would have seemed churlish to even hint that one of her problems might have been that she was lavishing all the potential profit on fattening up her guests.

In recent weeks Doreen had had a late booking from a group of Americans who then failed to show. In a village of only a dozen or so houses it did not prove difficult to track the errant walkers down to a neighbouring b&b.

"I rang and asked t'speak to Greta and she comes on phone and I says eeh, watcha doin there? I've two rooms waiting. She says 'that couldn't have been me'. I reels off er email address and she says 'oh, yes'. So I says that's you aint it and yer've cost me £100 because I've turned other folk away expecting yer. And she says ' I really don't know how that happened'. And I tell her 'I know how it happened. It's because you're Americans, that's how.' Haven't got a clue that lot."

Still, the stayaway Americans got off lightly compared to a pair of Japanese walkers who arrived late to Doreen's after losing their way. They told her they'd stopped to ask a farmer where Butt House was. According to Doreen he'd retorted: "Yer found way t'Pearl Harbour. Yer can blooddy well find yer own way ter Keld."

A life of service

Stuffed with garlic mushrooms, freshly baked bread, suet pies as big as plates, topped off with something creamy and meringuey, our stomachs were screaming for the relief of lying horizontal. But it proved impossible to make an early exit to bed because as soon as dinner finished Doreen shushed us all into the lounge so she could take our breakfast orders.

She pulled up her chair in front of the only exit, leaning her chunky arms on the sofa, and, wielding the notebook like a weapon, defied us to turn down the chance to enjoy more of her famed Yorkshire hospitality.

While others mithered over another long list of choices – a straining stomach is not the best starting point for predicting what you may fancy next – we studied the framed photos on the walls.

Many showed Doreen with various Conservative prime ministers and grandees, including a shot of her at William Hague's wedding. She was not only, it turned out, a legendary landlady but also the lynchpin of the local Conservative Party, able to get things done that had thwarted others for generations, simply by picking up the phone to one of her friends in power.

Apparently Keld owed its new telephone lines to Doreen's efforts, while a tv documentary on William Hague showed him sitting at her kitchen table where she dispensed common sense advice to the politician (and probably chocolate cake too).

More relevant to walkers such as ourselves, Doreen was the author of a slim but invaluable accommodation guide to the Coast to

Coast, detailing all the places en route where walkers could stop, though none could match her own fantastically over-the-top style. During our walks it was the best guide of its kind.

Sadly, Doreen's own chocolate-cake making, storytelling days, ended in 2007 when ill health forced her and husband Ernest to give up Butt House.

I'm glad we got the chance to stay there and it won't surprise you to learn that next morning the mountain of scrambled eggs on our plates had been made with full cream. If today's Coast to Coasters are missing out on such hospitality, Doreen's retirement is at least good news for wayward American tourists and the coronary units of hospitals up and down the country.

Chapter 9: Between two worlds, Clay Bank Top – Ingleby Cross

What goes up must come down, and up and down, and up and down. No fewer than seven times in a single day as it turns out.

This next stretch on the Coast to Coast is a perfect switchback of climbs and descents as the route navigates the edge of the most northern ridge of the Cleveland Hills. For a good few hours it offers a heady sense of being between two worlds: on one side the wild empty spaces of moorland; on the other a sheer drop to the flatness of fields and villages, and, beyond, the smoking chimneys of Middlesborough, Redcar, and the chemical plant at Seal Sands.

But I'm getting ahead of myself.

Having introduced you to a Coast to Coast legend in the last chapter I ought to mention Dave, who we found on TripAdvisor and stay with at the end of the hike to Clay Bank Top.

The reviews were fulsome. For £35, Dave was said to not only provide bed and breakfast but lifts from and back to the Coast to Coast and his home at Dromonby Bridge. Since there was nothing else there, he also offered lifts to and from the local pub.

All true: Dave does indeed pick us up from Clay Bank in a red Mercedes that had seen almost as many summers as us. He also runs us to the Blackwell Ox Inn in nearby Carlton which, strangely for a country pub in one of the most non-nonsense parts of the UK, specialises in Thai food.

But then, frankly, everything about this particular stay has an edge of strangeness. First Dave himself, who looks more like he sessions for Status Quo than a traditional landlord: long grey wavy hair held off his face with a shoelace. Dave tells us he'd spent 30 years as a builder then decided it was time to start working from home, but failed to make it as a pig farmer. Providing digs for people must have been the next best thing.

In true builder style, nothing about his place is quite finished. The lovely arched window in our bedroom gives real grandeur to the house's front facade but can't actually be opened. While the side window is crumbling and can't be closed.

Tea on arrival comes from a huge urn in the dining room: the same urn from which the 'freshly brewed coffee' promised by the website dispenses hot water to mix with instant powder from a jar. And don't get me started on the rusting state of the golden syrup pot, the tablespoon I'm supposed to eat cereal with, or the mansize shampoo which is the only toiletry on offer in the bathroom.

I sound churlish, and I don't mean to be because, actually, the whole stay and the transportation are great value from someone trying very hard indeed. Just don't arrive expecting White Company bath products.

Coffins

The fact that Dave has eight of us to ferry back to the route means it is before 9am when the red Merc drops us back in the car park; that perfect time of day when everything is fresh and new and the only people you meet en route are those who love the hills even more passionately than you do.

Hasty Bank is the first of the day's ascents, a gentlish climb up a soft green bank of grass, and a chance to look back across the valley at yesterday's landscape. "Another thing we've learned along the way: always remember to stop and look at where you've been," Shushie says as we pause to gaze back at the brown line where Urra Moor began. "It looks different from where you've go to, yet it's the reason you got to where you are."

We both smile at the obviousness of her meaning.

At the foot of Hasty are a couple of memorials – the first of many we pass that day. One commemorates a parent who had walked the hills for 50 years: 'loved beyond years, missed beyond tears'. The second is to someone who died on the Lyke Wake Walk.

A word about the Lyke Wake, in case our weekend wandering is too tame for your taste. The Lyke Wake is a 40-mile crossing of the North Yorks Moors which spends some time shadowing the Coast to Coast. Appropriately, given you're supposed to complete it in under 24 hours, its symbol is a coffin – actually alluding to the idea of watching over (wake) a corpse (lyke).

More than one person has died attempting the challenge. I hope none of them was lulled into a false sense of security by the website of the Lyke Wake Club which, rather discouragingly, records that the fastest crossing took just 4 hours and 40 minutes and that the youngest person to complete this tough-man challenge so far was six years old.

Follow the flags

We are also on the Cleveland Way – three walks for the price of one. And very impressed by the way Cleveland has taken care to protect its hills from the onslaught of walkers who find the views from this lofty perch irresistible.

Way back in 1997 when we first walked these hills we spotted car-sized canvas sacks packed with stone boulders, apparently dropped by helicopters for there were no roads to have brought them. Sixteen years later those raw materials have been transformed into a flagstone path which keeps boots and dogs and the occasional mad cyclist out of the brush where birds are nesting. It is an impressive result.

And an interesting introduction to the Wainstones, which straddle the summit of Hasty Bank and also look exactly as if they have been dropped from on high by a giant hand: they are tumbled together, sharp-edged, on a colossal scale compared to the humans clambering over them.

In places huge boulders are perched on others and though they have almost certainly been there for centuries some of the configurations look so precarious I can imagine they might collapse at any time.

We edge our way through and over them and take time to sit on the rock shelves, enjoying the view out across all the places Shushie knows from the years her life was in Teeside. It is only when we descend the hill and look back we realise the stones are not some act of God but the hill revealing itself: turf and soil peeled back by the elements to expose the hard skeleton beneath the surface.

Our path drops down from the Wainstones to begin another climb up onto Cold Moor, carpeted in heather, with the inevitable grouse butts rising a little above their level, waiting for the 'glorious 12th' and a different kind of visitor.

From Cold Moor we ride the switchback to Cringle Moor via a promontory with another memorial – this time a seat dedicated to a local rambler named Alec Falconer who was instrumental in campaigning for the Cleveland Way to become a recognised path.

In front of his seat an old way-marker points to coastal resorts and Richmond, and the Dales, where we will head on our next walking weekend.

But there is no reference to any of the Coast to Coast's landmarks; Wainwright's walk, celebrating its 40th anniversary this year, is a mere whippersnapper compared to these ancient routes on the Cleveland cliff edge.

Missing in action

Other landmarks we recall from previous crossings are missing too. The Lord Stones cafe is shut and looks as if it will re-emerge in a far slicker, more commercial form than the humble stone shed we remember stopping at for refreshments. (The only time a cream tea has featured a puny squirt of aerated slop from a can sprayed onto a saucer; so perhaps this refurb is overdue.)

Also missing is the airfield which once ran like a scar across our next rise – Carlton Moor – though the patchwork shading of the plateau at the summit still hints of the gliders who lifted off from here to soar across the moors.

The final moor we cross on our almost-yellow brick road is Live Moor, bleak and empty despite its name, until it descends and for the first time since we started out there are trees, their branches flushed green at the tips with new growth. It is time to stop for a basic lunch of peanut butter and banana sandwiches cobbled together from what was on offer at breakfast that morning.

And time to say farewell to Roseberry Topping and the views out across Cleveland, as far as the horizon where even now there is still a suggestion of blue where land meets sea. We are almost one quarter of the distance into the Coast to Coast and we can still see the east coast.

We have spent all morning poised in a kind of no-man's land between, on one hand, beauty, space, freedom and the exhilarating sense of being above it all; on the other, spread out as far as our eyes can see the stage on which we live our daily lives: miniature homes and factories, shops, busyness, smoke and mirrors.

From up here it all looks so small and just a little crazy.

I think, as we descend, that the real trick would be to continue on the edge, living with a foot always in both worlds.

Unforgiving minutes, Live Moor to Ingleby Cross

Funny thing, time.

When your back is buckling under the weight of a pack containing Things You Absolutely Can't Do Without (change of clothes, soft shoes, maps, water bottle, space blanket and, yes, ok then, hair straighteners, conditioner and moisturiser) there seem to be at least twice as many minutes in every hour. The time to destination when you can ditch the pack in favour of those soft shoes drags as heavy as your screaming muscles.

At other times there are plainly fewer than 30 minutes in any hour. Such as from the moment you pass the halfway point in your holiday, or when you finally unwrap a chocolate bar you've been anticipating all day long. Gone before you've even licked your lips.

I mention this because once Shushie and I leave the Cleveland switchback to head down into Scugdale (a misnamed place if ever I heard one – it's a beautiful little backwater) time begins to speed up. It's as if even just knowing the walking is almost over for another weekend and we've got to head home shifts us into a different relationship with the clock.

Out on the hills (crippling backpacks aside) the hours stretch like a cat in the sunshine. Time has no meaning as the day unfolds in a promise of new sights and sounds and places; the space to talk and reflect or rest in silence.

Back home, time is more often than not an enemy; something we grapple with in order to get through The List; to survive the day intact in order that we can do it all again the next, and the next after that. It seems to me it's this sameness that explains why the days merge together so that time speeds by like scenes watched from the window of a high-speed train.

Not on that day though for dear old Scugdale seems to be hurrying us on.

From a handful of houses at Huthwaite Green we head up a farm track to ford Piper Beck into Clain Wood. The beck's banks are overrun with wild garlic, its tangy smell scenting the forest air, until we reached the wood proper and in place of garlic stalks are carpets of bluebells and wood sorell, primroses, forget-me-nots and celandine, dappled in the sunlight poking its way through tree tops.

The forest ends in a flight of wide steps which lift us onto a small summit with a bench positioned to offer a final view of the Cleveland Plain, half-obscured by the branches of trees reaching for the light.

Beyond this bench the Coast to Coast crosses a moorland road at Scarth Nick – unlike Scugdale a name that definitely suits the jagged gash between the hills. Apparently this route was once Britain's wild west: used by a particularly tough breed of Scots cattlemen, driving their herds south for hundreds of miles to London to satisfy England's taste for beef.

Now there's a journey that will have taken time.

Our path, however, continues westerly, climbing again, up alongside pasture to the top of Beacon Hill, which is notable mainly for its forest of aerials. And a BT sign on the wire fence whose tone is a cross between apologetic and hurt as it points out that we can't have the convenience of our mobile phones without the occasional inconvenience of an eyesore such as this one.

Beyond BT the path shoots down into Arncliffe Woods, via a series of frustrating zig zags which account for far too many of this day's total miles, without repaying our efforts with anything in the way of views, wildlife, interesting flora.

It isn't only the sameness of the scenery that is responsible for time speeding up. In the near distance the thunder of car tyres on the A19 is unavoidable and has the same effect on our pace as one of those go-faster rock anthems which you hear on the car radio and before you know it your foot is pushing harder on the accelerator.

There is one brief moment of respite when, finally, we clear the last of the trees and reach a row of small cottages. Outside one of them is a table and on it a wicker picnic basket, with a handwritten sign propped against the side. 'Home-made flapjacks: apple and cinnamon or fruit and nut flapjacks £1. Please help yourself.'

Their crumbly sweetness is the perfect tonic to our now-edgy mood.

And if you are reading this and happen to be someone whose home or business lies on the Coast to Coast – or indeed any popular walking route – let me encourage you to follow this example and set your own basket of baked goodies on the path outside where they will make the miles sweeter for any passing walker.

The first time we walked this leg of the Coast to Coast it was impossible to turn on the radio without hearing Elton John's *Candle in the Wind* tribute to Princess Diana, or to believe that the hills he was singing about, where her footsteps would echo, were anywhere other than those right in front of us: the beautiful, wild and majestic Cleveland Hills.

Another memory from that strange period in our national life comes back to me now: the reading on Time at Diana's funeral which ended with the words that 'for those who love, time is eternity'.

That's why the three days we're walking the Coast to Coast together last an eternity.

Remember me this way?

Memorials are much on our minds during those brilliant two days on the North Yorks Moors and Cleveland Hills – simply because there are so many of them. It's no exaggeration to say we see almost as many memorial plaques and benches and posts – and in one case a simple bouquet – as we see ancient standing stones.

Which makes me wonder why would anyone want to be their life to be celebrated in a crowded municipal cemetery when their memorial could be a lofty hilltop commanding views over several counties? Or a bench offering rest and the chance for a moment's reflection?

The more I think about it, the more I see that standing stones and these memorials have in common. For both are about showing the way.

For our ancestors those standing stones were there to show the way in the most literal sense, preventing passers-by from getting lost on the lonely moors.

For us, modern memorials to other people's lives are just as much about not getting lost – but in this case, not getting lost in our own stories. If anything serves to point a way to living life now - getting out there, breathing deep, taking time, enjoying the view, and engaging every single one of our senses to experience it all - it's these reminders that one day it will be over.

Away with the eagles

The other point about these memorials is that they're not to be found where most of spend most of our waking hours. I don't believe I've ever seen a plaque in a town centre to 'Maureen, who loved this branch of Marks & Spencer'; any more than I've seen a sagging sofa with the legend 'in memory of Steve who spent his happiest hours here' or an office photocopier dedicated to 'Sue who walked these corridors from dawn to dusk'.

Cheap shot I know, but you get my meaning. The places we love the most – and where others want to remember us – are so often in the great outdoors. The places where we can just be, rather than having to do. Places of peace, beauty, and almost always perspective, as we are reminded, briefly, that whatever may be preoccupying us there is always this bigger picture.

Throughout my life there have been few crises, losses or knockbacks that weren't a little soothed by taking them outdoors. I can still remember 30 years ago lying on my back staring up at a Saharan night sky and realising for the first time how infinitesimally small my life and therefore the problems I'd gone to Africa to escape from really were. Which sounds as if it ought to be the very opposite of reassuring, except that along with this sense of my own insignificance came a powerful, life-changing conviction that I was at the same time part of something totally vast and more incredible than my limited human mind could ever conceive.

So (with an understanding nod in the direction of the British climate) remind me exactly why don't we spend more time in those places we love?

I understand why people erect memorials but I've always been more drawn to Karen Blixen's view, expressed so beautifully in her *Letters from Africa*: *"If I know a song of Africa, of the giraffe and the African new moon lying on her back...does Africa know a song of me? Will the air over the plain quiver with a colour that I had on...or the full moon throw a shadow over the ground of the drive that was like me, or will the eagles of the Ngong Hills look out for me?"*

I'll settle for eagles.

Chapter 10: Slough of Despond? Ingleby Arncliffe – Danby Wiske

This isn't the first and won't be the last account of walking the Coast to Coast. We came across someone else's self-published story when we were staying with Doreen. To be honest, it made dismal reading.

The author and her husband had set out in pouring rain, walked in pouring rain, woke each day to pouring rain, and ended up skipping half of the later legs because they couldn't face wet boots and soggy sandwiches for one more day. For obvious reasons, the book was short on photos.

One advantage of doing the Coast by Coast by stages, as we are, is that each month's leg brings the possibility of different weather. We're not caught for days on end in a particularly stubborn weather front, as some of those we've already met en route have been – like that unfortunate author.

That said, at the very end of June it is our turn to run foul of the weather Gods.

We drive north again on a ridiculously unseasonal grey, cold and wet Friday, rain hammering on the windscreen, and no prospect of any let up.

It seems somehow appropriate for a leg of this 190-mile long distance walk that Wainwright reserves some of his most eloquent disdain for: 23 miles across the Vale of Mowbray from Ingleby Cross to Richmond which, he huffs, is at best 'tedious', at worst 'a Slough of Despond'.

Just listen to him: *"To walkers whose liking is for high places and rough terrain this will seem the dullest part of the whole walk…tedium grows apace and one plods onwards mechanically, head down, thinking nostalgically of places left behind. Although in the midst of a thriving husbandry, few people are seen; in fact one feels lonelier here than one does on the mountains. There is nothing to see, nothing worthy of illustration, nothing of interest to anyone but farmers. Walking as a pastime is unheard of and incomprehensible."*

Our plan is to ignore him entirely and embrace the Vale over two separate days as if it must have as much to offer as any other leg.

Down and out in January

This, you'll understand, is flying in the face of our own experience. Back in the late 1990s, when we first did the walk, we determined, rather whimsically, that it would be interesting to walk in every season. Why we thought January was a suitable month to walk the Vale of Mowbray is beyond me now, unless we were so thoroughly persuaded by Wainwright's damming verdict that we decided that as it was going to be so awful anyway we might as well make it the winter leg.

It did not disappoint: we clumped through mud, acquiring several extra inches of height (and considerable weight) through the stuff cloying to our boots; we saw not a soul nor any sign of welcome; and we finished the last five or so miles in pitch darkness, hoping not to stray in any beck or river. Because, of course, in January the days are short and even the most basic arithmetic should have told us that 23 miles of mud was going to need at least 8 hours of daylight.

This time, we're determined, will be different. Even if the driving rain suggested otherwise.

So what can I tell you about Friday's eight mile stretch from Ingleby to Danby Wiske?

I can say that it begins dramatically with a crossing of the A19, dodging lorries thundering madly north and south – as amazed, I suspect, to see two hooded and jacketed walkers scurrying in their path as we are to discover how wide the road is when you are on foot.

We are spared a sticky end but, as the walk continues to gain in popularity, it can only be a matter of time before someone realises if they don't put a footbridge over one of the region's fastest and noisiest highways it won't only be hedgehogs they're scraping off the road.

I can also tell you that the sodden road and path verges smell of cabbage kept too long in the pan; that in one place we smell, long before we can see, two dead sheep carcasses, picked off by the weather no doubt; that Wainwright is wrong about there being no height: there is – from the lines of pylons astride the fields like malevolent giants; and equally wrong about it being featureless. We see several features of the what-were-they-thinking variety: a stone great dane outside a farmhouse, plastic rats and a skull nailed to a gate, the name of a farm spelt out in red foam letters more suited to a child's nursery. Weird lot those Mowbrayers.

And yet that's not the whole story.

Our guide book directs us through narrow woodlands and along field edges where, despite their soaking, the hedgerows are a riot of yellow vetch, purple clover, daisies and the pink blush of dog roses.

The waist-high fieldgrasses have the same effect on our clothing and boots as if we've simply walked into a car wash. And yet whenever the rain eases their leaves are covered in sparkling droplets of water, like fields of moonstone.

Everywhere the barley is growing high and as the breeze carries the wind through it, ripples move the stalks in a wave from one horizon to the other.

Above all, we are outdoors, doing what we love, breathing the air, getting up close and personal with a landscape that puts food on the table, chewing the cud with each other as determinedly as the cows in fields we pass through.

There are worse things than being soaked. But there are few better things than walking the Coast to Coast with my sister.

Postscript

We reach Danby Wiske with half an hour to spare before the taxi I've arranged to meet and take us back to Shushie's car is due.

Which means there is time to check out another Coast to Coast landmark, the White Swan, dismissed by Wainwright as a place where 'no-one wants to know'.

Times had already changed by the time we reached Danby Wiske on our second crossing – though not by much. Where, in Wainwright's day, the most the White Swan could rustle up was a mean bag of crisps, by 2005 you could eat and sleep there.

Eating, however, involved ordering your meal the moment you walked through the door, before being allowed to offload your backpack and go to your room.

It then meant coming downstairs at precisely the time you'd booked for to find your meal already plonked on the table, growing colder and stickier by the minute.

A most peculiar way to attract all that potential passing trade.

Happily, the bar we step into in 2013 has been refurbished and boasts a line of certificates for the quality of its ales.

It is also, promisingly, full of walkers – most of them staying the night, and though they are being asked to book a table we are relieved to see they are not being asked to say at 3pm exactly what they want to eat 4 hours later.

I gather the White Swan has changed hands again – three summers ago or so.

Nevertheless, there is a brief moment of deja vu when the friendly barman tells us with a straight face: "Sorry not to have your tea. We're right out of hot water."

Clearly we should have ordered it before setting out.

Chapter 11: Fields of gold, Danby Wiske - Bolton-on-Swale

Saskia the taxi driver and I had some trouble understanding each other on the phone.

"Richmond Market Square at 9.30. I don't know it too well. Where do you suggest we wait?"

"You know cock, the big cock?"

"The big cock?"

"Cock. Cock." Saskia repeated, beginning to gurgle with laughter. "You know, eet tells the time."

"Ah, *clock*."

"Sorry, my English is not so good," said Saskia.

More tortuous logistics

Where does the lovely Saskia come into our story? Afraid it's back to our contrary decision to travel east to west, putting us normally out of the orbit of the Coast to Coast's two excellent luggage-carrying-accommodation-booking services, Sherpa and Packhorse.

For this particular leg, having decided we need a break from those crippling rucksacks, this means:

Friday: drive from Leighton Buzzard to Ingleby Cross, walk 8 miles to Danby Wiske, take taxi from Danby back to car at Ingleby, drive to Richmond to stay the night

Saturday: take taxi back to Danby, walk 14 miles to Richmond and stay night again

Sunday: walk 11 miles from Richmond to Reeth, catch bus back to Richmond, drive back to Leighton Buzzard.

Simples.

From Russia with love

So Saskia is our second lift of the weekend and as unlike traditional taxi drivers as her Russian homeland is unlike Richmond. For one thing, she arrives underneath the clock not with a toot but with a huge smile and a big wave, as if she was on a day out with old friends.

Hers is one of those wonderful stories that make you wonder why you effort so much when life is just as likely to sneak up and blindside you.

A civil servant in Russia, divorced with a young son, Saskia tells us she thought she'd pretty much got it together when she took a week off to go and stay with her brother in the city.

"I meet my husband there. He is tourist and asks a question and so it goes. We see each other that week then he goes home to Richmond. Then contact, contact, contact," she says a little shyly. "Then we get married.

"If you ask me seven years ago if I am living in England and driving a car as my work I would not believe you."

She misses home. She even misses the -25degree winters she says, but we don't need Saskia's assurances that she's happy because we can feel it in her laughter and curiosity and in her refusal to take a penny more than she quoted us, even though her cab's clock says different.

She's a total gem.

The bread bowl

For us, the day is to be a love story of a different kind, walking the fields of our childhood. It may have been farmland and flatness to Wainwright; for Shushie and I it is the landscape we used to play in, far out of the sight of parents who'd done the same when they were young, building dens from hay bales, hide and seek in cornfields that outgrew us, stealing cattle feed for make-believe picnics.

Yesterday's rain is gone, the sky is light, the field grasses dry, and every tractor and baler in the county is already out in fields ripe with sunny buttercups and purple clover.

As they mow and bale in ever decreasing circles the shorn fields release clouds of summer perfume. The air is heady with the scent of hay and before long the temptation to lie down in it, breathe in the dusty freshness, gazing up through feathery cornstalks at the moving canvas of the sky, becomes irresistible.

Such a simple pleasure, and yet I'm not sure either of us has lain down in the corn since we were kids.

So, Wainwright's opinions notwithstanding, here is something the Vale of Mowbray *does* bring to the Coast to Coast party – a chance to rediscover some of those small pleasures that were a taken-for-granted part of our generation's growing up, roaming the fields with gangs of friends, peeling a few seeds of ripe wheat to chew on, paddling in streams.

We hold buttercups under our chins, swing on a gate, run our hands across the tickly corn heads, and if we'd jam jars we'd have probably made perfume from the confetti of wild rose petals at our feet: these fields might be England's bread basket but on this proper summer's day they are our play park too.

My inner country girl is having a field day, literally, even more so when we arrive at West Farm where the cows are wearing large necklaces with bells on around their necks.

As Shushie struggles with the gate a wiry old man dressed in blue overalls calls out to us from the edge of the field.

"Need help lasses?"

"We're there thanks," I say, and then, because he looks as if he's happy to be distracted, "It's a long time since I've seen cows with bells on."

Blue overalls looks at me a little oddly. As does Shushie.

"Those are transponders. It's how we milk now. All done with robots."

Not quite everything stays the same then.

Return of the nogs

Wainwright's original book in 1973 devoted a whole page to the issue of rights of way, particularly in this rural part of the world where the only way to avoid road walking is through the fields of a dozen or more farmers. Spurred on by a succession of obstacles, including bulls, Wainwright reported his experiences 'in gruesome detail'to the then North Riding County Council, promising future travellers should have 'a smoother passage'.

Just the same, it's clear to us as walkers that we have a different agenda from those who are 'custodians' of the land. While we treat the rights of way with respect, sticking to tracks, leaving nothing but the lightest imprint of our boots on grass that will spring back up, some farmers suffer no such compunction. How many times have you seen a farm *without* its own equipment graveyard, littering the fields and road verges with rusting machinery, pyramids of tyres, empty feed sacks blown around?

Then, of course, there is their adversarial attitude to the wildlife which we regard with such joy. This is hunting country and shooting country – and all day long we hear the staccato retort of gunfire coming from the forests and distant farms.

I'm inclined to forgive them this noggish behaviour having seen at close quarters the relentless hours and effort that farming demands. But still, it's lovely to come across a place like Stanhow Farm where the buttercups and clover we've been following all morning suddenly burst into field bouquets of scabious and cornflower, dog roses and forget-me-nots, poppies and foxgloves.

Damselflies the colour of shimmering peacock feathers move like darts through this flowery paradise.

Along one field edge is a noticeboard explaining the work the farmer has done to improve the environment for wildlife – and walkers. Plus a comments book and blunt pencil, wrapped in polythene inside an old sandwich box, so we add our thanks to others left by Coast to Coasters from all over the globe.

Just the same, that uneasy stand-off between landowners and walkers is evident in a number of less than positive comments about overgrown paths and rotting stiles, and pinch-passageways through hedges that are accessible for only the slimmest of walkers. Stanhow is being blamed for the sins of the many. Just as there are no doubt noggish walkers causing headaches for farmers, who give the rest of us a bad name.

Bolton

Three hours into the day's walking the route crosses a road and dips into the fields of Laylands Farm to follow the meandering route of Bolton Beck, a lazy stream bordered by the tallest cow parsley plants we've ever seen. Truly, there must be something in that beck water.

After three fields the tower of Bolton-on-Swale Church is a clear landmark to leave the beck and head into the village which boasts one of the few manmade points of interest on this section.

Bolton's St Mary's Church is the final resting place of one Henry Jenkins, who clearly had whatever the cow parsley is having for, according to an ugly monument in the churchyard, Mr Jenkins lived to be 169 years old. Doubt ye not, for this remarkable feat was documented towards the end of his life when it emerged Jenkins could remember being sent as a 12-year-old lad with a cartload of arrows to meet the Earl of Surrey's army on its march north to fight the Battle of Flodden. That means he was born in 1500.

Bolton-on-Swale is missing a trick, I think, not bottling whatever is in the beck and selling it to those of us for whom even 169 years will not be enough time to walk all the fields of gold.

Chapter 12: What we know about losing the way, Bolton-on-Swale - Richmond

And then we get lost.

Not life or death lost like Emilia Earhart flying off the radar, never to be seen again. Just common or garden messing-it-up and heading-in-the-wrong-direction lost.

The guide book has less than a paragraph of directions to get us on the right route from Bolton-on-Swale to our next watering hole, Catterick Bridge. And I've been too confident about this weekend's legs to hassle the local library for an Ordnance Survey map.

Basic mistake, further compounded by the sort of silly errors we ought not still to be making after 16 years of walking weekends:

- assuming, because we can see other footpaths and other walkers, that they are on our route and we only have to follow them;

- getting flustered and blundering ahead when the description in the guidebook doesn't quite match what we can see instead of stopping and regrouping.

If you want the life learning in this then I'd say don't assume you need to follow the crowd, and, though we've been taught there are no wrong decisions, only 'learning opportunities', the truth is sometimes your best choice is to stop where you are for a bit and look around.

Coming full circle

On this particular day our come-uppance is a disused quarry, from which a path is supposed to take us to the Swale – our first encounter with a river that is going to accompany us into the heart of the Dales many miles ahead.

Don't ask me why we decide to ignore the book, cross a busy main road and choose to see a very much active quarry as our destination. We walk one long side, and then the second long side, ignoring the little voices in our heads that ask why the guidebook hasn't mentioned the leisure routes and wildlife trails criss-crossing this part of the world.

The path finally leads us out of this nature reserve, to a narrow country lane which then takes us into a village. We are not about to make the other mistake of the lost and proud (see 'Why men don't ask for directions'). The first person we see, we ask the way.

Catterick? Head down the main road then right onto that other main road and look out for a footpath sign.

Forty-five minutes and two miles after our disused quarry moment Shushie ventures: "This looks familiar. Haven't we been here before?"

Of course we have. We've walked in a huge circle. And now we come at it again we can clearly see that first time around we missed a small gap in the hedge leading directly down to the river's edge.

One more piece of advice, if your gut's telling you that something's not right, trust me, something's not right.

Follow that river

Once we find the Swale it is full steam ahead with a lightness of heart that comes from knowing that we'll be following this clear, excitable river not just to Catterick but onto Richmond and then into Swaledale and the Yorkshire Dales proper. So long as it is in our sights we can't go wrong.

That's the theory anyway.

It is easy walking along the lush and overgrown riverbank, sometimes glimpsing, sometimes hearing the white water which led the Romans to name Catterick for its cataracts. Except for another hairy road crossing in Catterick – where we also register some small satisfaction at seeing the Bridge House Hotel is up for sale. If you can't make it on a busy road junction opposite the race course, close to the A1 and on the doorstep of a major military garrison, then you must be doing something wrong.

Soundproofing your rooms mightn't be a bad place to start.

Between Catterick and Richmond there are more fields and the route climbs high above the Swale to take in the site of a former hospital at St Giles, and from there through more fields into the village of Colburn where, on the last Saturday in June, in full sun, the village pub has a sign on the door saying it does not open until 7pm.

We begin to see more Coast to Coasters heading the other way which is puzzling, so late in the day, until we realise they've probably spent the afternoon exploring Richmond and are heading onto Bolton-on-Swale to notch up a few of the 23m total distance covered by this Vale of Mowbray section to give themselves a more manageable distance the next day.

Wainwright recommends you stop overnight in Richmond and make the most of the chance to rest and reprovision in the only town of any size en route.

We of course have done better and are spending two nights in this fascinating town, though that post-lunch detour means we again arrive after the shops have shut.

Probably just as well: for such a relatively small town to have two decent secondhand bookshops, a lively craft market that's open seven days a week, plus at least a dozen tea shops, is asking for trouble.

Richmond

Wainwright made much use of his sketchbook when he stopped in Richmond, full of historic stone buildings, cobbled streets and narrow alleys. The whole place is dominated by the Norman castle, perched on a cliff above the Swale, and visible for miles around.

But the Coast to Coast is a bit of a tease when it comes to both castle and Richmond itself. You see them almost before you reach Catterick Bridge yet they seem to remain forever in the distance as you circle around, never quite knowing how far there is left to go.

Close to the town the path passes the ubiquitous sewage works then follows the A6136 for a few steps.

It takes Shushie and I a moment to realise the traffic on the road has stacked up behind a white car, stationery in the middle of the road. A blonde woman is hanging out of it waving and shouting 'You made it, you made it to here!"

The lovely Saskia. Proving once again she's not just any taxi driver: she's Top of the Taxi Cabs.

On the beach

It is gone five when we finally get a proper look at Richmond, peering through a hedge to find ourselves directly under the castle ramparts. There are only two things now on the 'to do' list after eight hours walking: get our boots off and find the cold cider we were unable to buy in Colburn.

We cross Richmond Bridge and head down to a beach made of bleached boulders where a few people are hauling red and yellow canoes from the water.

The Swale is bright silver in the late afternoon sun, light dancing off the clear water as it gurgles its way east. Somewhere up beyond the ramparts church bells mark the quarter hour. We hear them chime twice more before reluctantly agreeing that our feet – and our full-up hearts – have had enough cool-water therapy. It's beginning to worry me a little that the best and most memorable moments on this walk all seem to involve NOT walking.

Just cold cider to go then, and we know exactly where we're going to drink it: back at 66 Frenchgate, the brilliant b&b we'd been recommended to use in Richmond.

Frenchgate guest house not only has a charming owner in Ralph (whose modest answer to our question about whether he'd been running the place for long is 'oh no, only 12 years'); it also has the most amazing picture window from its dining room and lounge, looking out across the Swale, the Vale, and Richmond's clutter of rooftops and back gardens clinging to the cliffside.

Cold cider, awesome view, and upstairs, waiting for us, bath, shower, chocolates on the pillows and Yorkshire tea in our cosy room with a view under the eaves.

Does it get any better?

Chapter 13: Highs and lows, Richmond - Reeth

Ah, how we British love to celebrate failure. You'll find Robert Willance's name on guest houses, shops and streets in Richmond town, yet this 17th century lead magnate is famous for nothing more worthy than falling 200 feet off a cliff and living to tell the tale.

In case you're tempted to feel sorry for him you should know that most accounts suggest Willance was fairly full of himself – enough to ignore common sense and head out on horseback to check his many business interests in thick fog. And then to override the infinitely wiser instincts of his poor horse, who faltered as they bumbled through fog close to Whitecliff Scar. Willance spurred the mare on, right over the edge.

Every time I hear about Willance's Leap it's the horse I feel sorry for. Especially as Willance compounded his disregard for the poor animal by slitting open its body in order to keep his own shattered leg warm while he waited for help.

Why a town with so many alternative claims to fame should even nod in the direction of bull-headed Bob I don't know. On the other hand, his misfortune probably edges the news that one of Europe's first gas works was built in Richmond in 1830.

Wainwright was here

On the way out of Richmond, past tall houses and allotments, there's evidence that the town may be getting wise to the fact that in 2013 Wainwright is likely to do them more good than Willance.

Alongside the path there's a bench bearing a quote from the original Coast to Coast book, describing the 'thrilling view' as you approach 'a town unlike others…rich in the relics of the past'.

Close by, an advertising board for a local hostelry advises passers-by that there is a bar where Coast to Coasters can meet and compare notes. Judging from the number of people we are to pass throughout the course of this day, it will be more packed than a walker's rucksack.

For a while the path leaves the gentle downs above the Swale and the road linking Richmond and the Dales, and heads into Whitecliff Wood which is as garlicky as every other wood we have passed through on this stretch of the walk. But ancient too, for there are faces and twisted limbs in the tree roots.

We barely glance at Willance's Leap but set our faces in the direction of a succession of dales farms, through which the Coast to Coast passes, hugging stone walls, passing through narrow stiles, a breath away from where sheep are being herded off the slopes and into barns.

I don't want to think about why that might be. One thing our walks across England have taught us is that while we enjoy this intermittent contact with the English landscape of storybooks and paintings, of our childhood memory and a thousand patriotic songs, for more than six months of each year these fields are wild and the weather brutal and unforgiving. Those who farm it cannot afford sentiment – or, I suppose, the luxury of getting attached to fluffy things.

New pastures

The Swale valley is wide, gently curving into the heart of the Dales, towards Reeth – our target for this day and a village that sees itself as the real Dales gateway. As ever, our instinct is to follow that curve on a clear path that sweeps ahead, following one side of the valley on a shallow gradient.

Oddly, however, the guide book wants us to leave this obvious path at a cairn and head down through a field to cross the wooded Clapgate Beck – a name which surely belongs in fairytales –and then a series of fields thick with buttercups ending in a small road and from there into Marske.

Not a step of it is familiar, and yet we've walked the Coast to Coast before. Presumably, mistakenly, on that path along the valley side?

Which only goes to show that you are only lost if you believe yourself to be so. A bit like that dandelion analogy: whether you see a weed or a splash of gold or a salad determines what story you tell yourself about the humble yellow flower. We did not know we were 'lost' so we just carried on walking and loving it.

Lost again?

There is less to love about the steep climb out of Marske which is as pretty and deserted as every other village we've seen. But it has a sting in the tail: 'a stiff pull' according to our guide book; a cruelly long bit of road walking according to us. All those colourful fields brimming with life and colour and summer scents have spoiled us for even the smallest stretch of tarmac, and this one goes on – and on – and on.

The coast to coasters continue coming towards us in droves, in twos and fours and even the occasional five or six, stretching out for an early afternoon arrival in Richmond.

Finally, at the top of Marske, we're back off into the fields, and through cow pasture to Hollins Farm, where a series of huge yellow arrows are either intended to help walkers or to warn them off straying – probably both.

Shushie and I can't seem to help ourselves straying, and having walked around the farm boundary we're mystified by the next arrow on a gate. Does it mean hop over the locked gate into a field alongside a spinney, or carry straight on? We are unclear but also grown wiser over the course of this weekend.

"Let's have a coffee stop. Just sit and think about it for a minute," I suggest.

It takes us ages to even notice that another group of walkers has appeared and is heading where we have just come from. Since we hadn't heard them come from behind us that can only mean they have indeed hopped over the fence beside the wood. Sorted.

As I said, sometimes the correct response is not to do anything except sit and wait for the answer to appear.

The Nun's Chorus

Should you be thinking you may one day walk the Coast to Coast let me just say that this stretch, from Richmond to Reeth is one to truly savour. Do not rush. It may only be farmland but every inch of it is a reminder of life's exuberance. What is it Khalil Gibran says: 'life's longing for itself'.

From Hollins there are more fields down to the remote cottage at Ellers, a splash of green at the lowest point of acres of mown hay.

Regretfully, our bellies still full of Ralph's golden scrambled egg, we have to bypass a new cafe which has opened up at a farm on the edge of Marrick. 'Elaine's' is broadcast on the side of a barn and a series of boards and I'm certain is as wholesome and generous as only a Yorkshire farmhouse can be.

Our plan is to survive on coffee and a couple of gingerbread men from the Richmond bakery until we reach Reeth with its profusion of tea shops. So we pull up through another field and find ourselves entering the boundary of another farm, this time with a slight air of not really wanting walkers to be here at all. Every post bears a reminder about sticking to the path.

Given that this is another of those almost picturesquely messy farms, with derelict barns and gates hanging off posts, abandoned troughs and scrubby soil, I don't think there's any damage walkers might inflict to rival the farm's lack of care for itself.

But we do what we're told and follow the farm track into a sleeping Marrick, and then out the other side into Steps Wood where the path suddenly becomes stepped.

This is the Nuns' Causeway or Nunnery Steps which were, bizarrely, actually constructed by the nuns of Marrick Priory. There was me thinking nuns were all about quiet contemplation and praying for our souls, and it turns out that this bunch spent their time lugging rocks up a hill to create the 375-step passageway between village and priory.

A Yorkshire Sunday

The Priory and its steps are our last landmark before rejoining a virtually empty Dales road and later, the Swaleside path, on our way into Reeth, via the largest cycling rally I have ever seen.

It's perfect cycling weather, a mix of suspicious skies followed by bursts of sunshine. For us too, the perfect backdrop for a Yorkshire afternoon, to sit and enjoy the cream tea we've been promising ourselves. The icing on the teacake is a brass band tuning up to perform on the village green.

I've mentioned that Reeth has disappointed us in the past – particularly when it comes to providing a civil bed and breakfast. It turns out its citizens are not great fans of cream tea either. Of the only two cafes in town doing cream teas one is shut 'on family matters'. The other is in a dip without a view and the scones and cream that turn up are in such miserly portions that there can be no doubt that the cafe is owned by southerners.

Still hungry, we go in search of more food, this time to Reeth Bakery which rates a name check on many Coast to Coast sites for its hearty rolls. We can vouch for their tastiness certainly, but here is a place that has sadly bought into its own publicity and thinks that £4 is a

Dipping a toe at Robin Hood's Bay

The first of many signposts – pointing the wrong way for us of course

A little bedtime reading for me at Broom House

Shushie meets Fat Betty .... Comments book in a farmer's field

Between two worlds in the Cleveland Hills

Fields of gold in the Vale of Mowbray

Wading the watershed

Cider and choccie in Orton

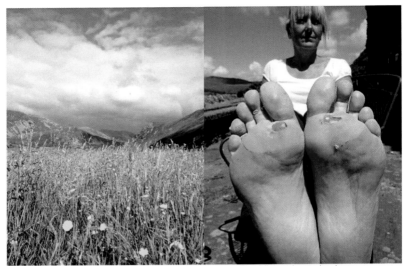

Stunning Ennerdale   The blisters I promised you

A

temporary memorial to our walk

reasonable price to pay for what is, after all, just a cheese roll. They even charge 45p extra for pickle.

But we find another bench, listening to the band, gazing up at the fields and farms of the Yorkshire Dales and munching on fresh rolls. There are worse ways to pass half an hour on a Sunday in June.

And there are plenty who agree with us. As we sit and watch an old second world war motorbike splutters past, its rider wearing army fatigues to match the era of his wheels. Perched behind his seat is a basket and in it an excited Jack Russell, barking its excitement at the day, and the sunshine, and the scene.

We know just how it feels.

Chapter 14: Heading for the Watershed

The hottest July in twenty-something years. Non-stop sunshine for three weeks. And the moment we head for the watershed all that stored-up, backed-up, malevolent rain begins to gush from the skies.

Let me explain about the watershed, which represents not just the midpoint of the Coast to Coast walk but the midpoint of England.

Between Reeth and Kirkby Stephen, where England's spine, the Pennine Way, runs north to south across the Yorkshire Dales, all the rivers and streams and (if you're from northern England, the becks and gills) collect and pause a moment to decide whether to flow east to the North Sea or west to the Irish Sea.

The watershed is England's collecting bowl, stunning in its remoteness, its wild farms and lonely stone cottages, its fissures and gorges and racing watercourses.

And soggy, sucking at your boots even on dry days. As for wet ones – beware, for in some places it is nothing but an oversized, seeping sponge, waiting for you to sink up to your armpits.

Bogged down

Our two previous crossings coincided with personal watersheds. In 1999, heading west, I was doing so having just left a marriage, home and job. Shushie would follow suit less than a year later.

In 2004 the shifts were more subtle, like the water perhaps, collecting out of sight beneath the surface as well as on top. Shushie had just celebrated one of those landmark birthdays at 40 while out of the blue the dream I'd had since childhood of writing a book had landed in my lap, setting in train a series of career shifts that would mean that by the end of that west to east crossing I could describe myself as a 'writer and workshop leader'.

I was struck, reading back my notes from that period, how positive the ageing process felt for us both at that point.

But as we drive north on a sunny Saturday afternoon at the end of July 2013 and I ask Shushie "How are we at the watershed again in our lives right now?" her answer is immediate: "midlife."

Caring around the clock for an increasingly helpless elderly parent; experiencing the freedom of not being full-time parents only to discover new tiny roots spreading around us as the children have children of their own; sleeping less, worrying more; noticing how set in their ways some of our friends are becoming and wondering if they say that about us too; grappling with the sort of stupid aches and pains we'd once have made jokes of, conscious that bits of our bodies – the knees we've punished through running and walking like this – don't want to play ball anymore.

Classic midlife, in other words, but, to be honest, not what I had expected.

We are, after all, the *Cosmopolitan* generation, brought up to believe we could have it all. And I don't remember anyone setting a time limit on that.

I think the thing collecting beneath the surface for both of us is a refusal to accept that this is how it has to be. Even if we don't yet know how it can be different. Maybe this watershed is a chance to follow the rivers' example and pause to collect ourselves, while we wait for life to show us in which direction to flow?

Wetter than a wet thing

Meantime, the actual watershed is waiting for us, ready to resume our long love-hate relationship: loving the wide skies, the height and views, and the relics of the land's industrial past that these days resemble sculptures.

Hating the apparent inevitability of low cloud, rain and obscured views, and therefore the challenge of trying to navigate a way through when you can scarcely see your boots, and know you'll end the day wetter than a dog who's chased a stick into the lake and is now rolling in a puddle.

As our taxi driver puts it as we rattle from Kirkby Stephen to Reeth after three inches of overnight rain has turned much of the narrow Dales road into a river: "They say when you can see the hills it's going to rain. And when you can't, it's raining."

Sticky toffee, Sea bass and Kirkby Stephen

Shushie says I should write more about where we eat and sleep on the Coast to Coast – and as I'm someone who skims through most of the Sunday supplements but can't ever pass by a restaurant or hotel review she's probably got a point. After all, many of the decisions we've made about bed & breakfasts and pubs have been based on other people's advice – either face to face on the walk, or via Trip Advisor – so it's good to give something back.

Sweet Ralph of Richmond Hill, for instance, at 66 Frenchgate, was a recommendation of the unlikely Swiss-Canadian lads we shared a meal with at Clay Bank Top. The same duo also gave us two recommendations for our current leg, in Keld and at Kirkby Stephen.

We lucked in at Keld Lodge – the lads' choice for 'best-en-route' – about which, more in a bit.

For Kirkby Stephen they suggested the Old Croft House, where we'd stayed previously. However, the summer holiday season is now in full swing so of course this is booked out.

Let me not pass by, though, without telling you that here is a b&b crammed with character, boasting loads of lovely antiques, a suit of armour in the hallway and fantastic food. What singled it out for us were the bathroom shelves groaning with every imaginable lotion and potion that a footsore walker might need if they are to hit the track again the next day. And A FOOT SPA.

Definitely extra Brownie points.

So it was over to TripAdvisor and via a number of 'no vacancies' to the promising-sounding Jolly Farmers.

But what's in a name? Now I think about it there are few folk so miserable as farmers, trying to scrape a living in the face of the even less jolly folk at Tesco forcing them to accept peanuts for produce they've invested a year of labour into.

Maybe this b&b had dropped its jollyness in sympathy…

Love what you do

There are some who choose to run b&bs because, having walked or journeyed themselves, they are convinced they can do it better. Let's call them the foot spa brigade.

There are others, like Dave at Clay Bank Top, who simply want a way of making a living from working at home.

There are those who dream of relocating to the landscape they love and see a b&b as their passport to making it happen. (Sadly, in our experience, many of these fizzle out in the face of the huge amount of work involved in cleaning up, being nice to people who know you live in fear of a bad review on TripAdvisor, and the torture of realizing you may look but still cannot touch the landscape because you're chained at home waiting for folk to show up.)

There are also the Ralphs who actually love people and would happily spend time sharing stories even if they weren't being paid for it. Shushie reminded me that Ralph said at least three times how much fun this kind of 'work' is, which endears him to me even more since I've come to believe you should keep looking for your perfect work until you find the thing you would still turn up to do even if you weren't being paid for it.

But a b&b is also a business, and it was this category that The Jolly Farmers fitted into most neatly: a bustling, efficient, perfectly respectable business, where we were well-looked after, greeted with fresh scones in the lounge and the assurance in the hotel notes that 'numerous hairdryers are available on request'. But where it was all just a little too, well, business-like.

Class of its own

No doubt it was the relentless busy-ness of life back home that walking is our antidote for that hit a nerve here. If I want to bustle I can do that any hour of the day any day of the week thank you very much.

With a human turnover of more than a dozen people a day I'm sure time is often too short for more than a cursory hello. Yet we hadn't headed to the hills in order to have more of those slightly glazed-over conversations which characterise the over-busy lives we currently lead.

I think this was the first b&b where we had to show ourselves to our room on the second floor, whereas Ralph treated our arrival like the grand 'reveal' in a makeover show, waiting as expectantly as a proud parent to enjoy our reaction to the view from the rooms.

As we were finishing a generous breakfast on Sunday morning at the God-fearing hour of 8.30am the cereal boxes were already being marshalled back into cupboards. And as we waited for our taxi the housekeeper took the stairs to our room two at a time.

"Did you see them bustling about in the kitchen like bees on speed?" Shushie whispered as we left. "They'll have our beds stripped and the sheets in the machine already, you can count on it."

At £72 a night the Jolly Farmers was one of the best value b&bs so far and, to be fair, the latest page of its visitor's book showed others praising it fulsomely: 'best b&b on the Coast to Coast so far' and 'hard to beat' read two of the entries.

Just the same, for us it was a bit like the head girl in school: admirable and good at what it does but nowhere near as much fun as the rest of the class.

A taste for the Black Bull

Kirkby Stephen itself has always seemed to us one of those places that disappoint slightly by promising more than they deliver. But this time it did have one treat up its sleeve: on our landlady's recommendation we booked dinner at the Black Bull hotel.

Previously we'd struggled to get a good meal in Kirkby – though the other high street hotel in town can at least take credit for being the first to introduce us to true Cartmel sticky toffee pudding – once tasted, forever smitten. (And, by the by, the perfect dish to represent Kirkby since its colour and texture *exactly* mirror the crumbly, mahogany-coloured terrain of the watershed above the town.

The Black Bull on a Saturday night does not have a table until 8.45 but, readers, it is well worth the wait. We dine from the two-courses for £16 menu, Shushie on steak, me on succulent seabass, with perfect vegetables, homemade chips and sauteed potatoes, followed by heavenly lemon cheesecake and ginger biscuit ice cream – undoubtedly some of the most imaginatively served and best tasting grub we've had on this Coast to Coast crossing.

In a town with half a dozen tea shops that fail to rise above the mediocre, the smell of frying from three chippies pervading the air, and a host of vintage and gift shops that are tantalisingly always closed, the Black Bull delivers.

It is almost enough to make us review our feelings about the town.

Until we wake the next morning to torrential rain.

Chapter 15: The Colour Purple, Reeth – Keld

Have I mentioned that it is raining?

Oh, OK then, but I still want you to understand that this isn't any old rain but a month's worth or more in one go, tumbling down into the dales where we'll be walking next; turning the gentle gills to churning rivers of chocolate as they sweep away the peaty soil scoured from the tops.

Our cab – which is actually a minibus – from Kirkby to the starting point at Reeth has seen better days. Which adds to the impression we are riding a water chute at the theme park, hurtling through torrents of water where the rainfall has proven too intense for the rivers to contain and poured straight down the path of least resistance to the narrow dales road.

Even the ducks can't work out where they are supposed to be and are paddling in stone-walled fields.

As we rattle through Keld – pausing to drop-off our bags at the Lodge where we'll be stopping tonight – I wonder how a family of campers reacted when they unzipped their tent door this morning to find the pretty River Swale they'd pitched alongside has swollen to a seething mess just a few inches from the canvas.

If they left their boots outside last night they are in trouble.

Twice stung

One more word on logistics before we move onto the day's walking business: our unscheduled taxi flume comes in at £61, though the lovely driver insists on capping it at £50 and refuses a tip. An ouch moment, naturally, but given it has taken him an hour to carry us through the wet, and he now has to retrace his tyre tracks for the next job, not unreasonable.

The advantage of this slow start to the day's walking turns out to be that it gives the rain a chance to stop.

Don't get me wrong. As we set out from Reeth down the narrowest of overgrown lanes, everything is sopping. Which means within five minutes we are too. And stung by nettles: it turns out the nettles are bred as hardy as everything else in Yorkshire and are more than a match for mere clothing.

The sky is still heavy with cloud but as our path opens up the landscape is doing its very best to compensate with delicate lilac harebells and the first purple flushes of heather.

I'll admit it: Shushie and I started the day in a funk as soon as we saw it was raining. Yet again.

Working, juggling, efforting through all that sunshine for days on end and now when we finally have the chance to get away and do something nice for ourselves, the skies turn to lead and the ground to mush. In both of us there is, I think, an unspoken 'it's not fair' - the sun bloody well ought to shine on the righteous.

Yet the sight of all that purple brings me back to myself. What is it Celie says in *The Colour Purple*? "I think it pisses God off if you walk by the colour purple in a field somewhere and don't notice it."

The weather isn't personal and whether we walk through sun or rain, we'll try to keep on reminding ourselves to notice the beauty.

A choice of routes

If you are walking the Coast to Coast you have a choice of routes between Reeth and Keld (and Keld and Kirkby Stephen come to that): the guide books do not entirely trust their readers with the cross-country route.

Dear Terry Marsh, who did such a great job of getting us off the roads in the Vale of Mowbray, urged us to stay low on the 'royal road' of riverside walking to Keld, warning that the high-level route can be confusing with 'considerable potential for error'.

But we've passed this way twice before and will have none of it. While the lower route is indeed through lush countryside, Shushie and I have always found as much beauty – and a great deal more interest – in the rugged valleys of this area, where the hillsides are scarred by mine workings and ruined buildings stand like sentries alongside now quiet gulleys.

Since Roman times the valleys we'll pass through on the high-level route – Swinnergill, Gunnerside, Hard Level Gill and Cringley Bottom – were mined for lead needed for shipbuilding, plumbing and rooves – especially the great church and castle rooves.

Indeed by the 19th century Britian was producing more than half the world's lead, and Yorkshire's mines were at the very centre of the industry, using gunpowder to expose the mineral veins.

I had wondered before at the meaning of the name of the first of these old mine workings reached on this leg – Surrender mine. I still don't actually know why it's called that but thinking about the men who worked the poisonous lead it feels fitting.

While the mine owners grew wealthy, their employees labored night and day for weeks at a time in cramped and dangerous conditions, often underground, too poor to own the tools they worked with so forced to spend their wages on hiring them from agents.

And it wasn't only the conditions. In a lead mine the very air they breathed was slowly killing them. Surrender hope all you who entered here.

More mines

A glimpse of sun at Surrender Mine is enough to persuade us to take a break – though we've forgotten to pack a flask for this weekend and, after failing to bring a map on the last leg, resolve our overloaded brains would benefit from us writing a List of Things To Bring.

Then it's on, further up the valley to Old Gang Mine, whose ruins stretch even further across the sides of the dale, and in one place burrow darkly into the hillside – as the men who worked this mine once did.

But on this day there are no ghosts. Indeed, there are no living either. They must all be on the low-level route for we have these ancient places to ourselves – apart from little families of grouse being shepherded off the path and away from us by clucking parents.

Beyond Old Gang we cross the gill back up into the heather, and from there to a strange wilderness where nothing seems to to be growing.

This is the place where gravel from the spoil heaps of the many mines was dumped – and an opportunity for the ever-gloomy Alfred Wainwright to lament "not a blade of grass nor a sprig of heather is visible in a vast desert of stones."

As unpromising as this interlude is, however, it also marks the 100-mile point for anyone coming from west to east, (and for us the 90-mile mark), so perhaps it is not all bad.

Into Gunnerside

When the miners weren't bombing these hills they were 'hushing' them. Which sounds a lot nicer than it looks.

Hushing involved damming the streams and then releasing the water with such force it scoured away the surface of the valley sides, creating huge ravines and exposing any mineral veins.

Our route into Gunnerside is down one of these ravines which, even a century after the mines were closed, still make the beautiful dales countryside look bruised and beaten-up.

But last night's rain has swollen Gunnerside Gill to a noisy torrent and, sitting with our egg sandwiches above it, it is possible to imagine a time when all of the stone ghosts will have crumbled into the water and even the scarred hills will be reclaimed by heather and rabbits.

We find a place where there are enough boulders to allow us to cross the gill without getting too damp and climb back out of yet another of these deep, narrow dales valleys, which channel away from the floor of Swaledale like probing fingers.

The last valley for the day is Swinnergill, described by Wainwright as 'grim and rather eerie', but by the time we reach it, at mid-afternoon, it is bathed in golden sunshine and completely delightful.

To add to our pleasure we encounter some of the only other walkers we'll meet on this day, and are therefore able to enlist their help in recreating a photo we'd had taken on our first Coast to Coast crossing at the end of the 1990s.

With the express purpose, of course, of contrasting and comparing.

Are we fitter more than a decade on? Stronger? Happier? More sure of ourselves?

I don't know, but I am willing to go so far as to say we are wiser. Certainly wise enough to welcome the sunshine and slow our steps to really appreciate the beauty of Swinnergill, with its endless cascade of waterfalls and splash pools, its flower-decked valley sides and soft mosses.

Even Crackpot Hall, once a handsome home for someone, has no trace of the sad decay and folornness that Wainwright detected when he devised the route. Rather, a young family are poking amongst its stones and what catches our eyes are the traces of decoration around the door lintel.

Lashings of ginger beer

From Swinnergill the route hits another landmark: imagine 'X' marking the spot where Wainwright's west to east route crosses the Pennine Way, running several hundred miles from north to south.

We scarcely register the moment, however, such is the noise coming from East Gill Force, hurling water from all the hills we've crossed down into the churning Swale. Its force is mesmerising, and in the sunshine the clouds of spray create a myriad rainbows.

How strange, really, to emerge into this other world of riverside benches and ice-cream eating tourists, after our lonely walk through the centuries.

More than any other dales village we know, Keld is a genuine outpost with a mere handful of houses, and only the shelves of a campsite office for reprovisioning.

Shushie and I are reluctant to let the day be over, so head into the campsite for bottles of cold ginger beer, which we drink, sitting in the garden outside, passing the time of day with other walkers, and blessing our luck to have seen so much of the sun in the end.

But the best is yet to come.

It turns out that Keld Lodge's transformation from youth hostel to walkers' fantasy is every bit as wonderful as we'd been promised.

Our room, on the corner of the first floor, looks out on two sides, across the gentle green sides of Swaledale. The shower is of mammoth proportions.

Downstairs, the restaurant offers the same blissful view as our bedroom and, just possibly, serves us the best meal we've eaten on the Coast to Coast so far: grilled Swaledale goat's cheese with walnuts, dates and honey dressing, beef pie made with Black Sheep Bitter, creme brulee with homemade shortbread, deconstructed lemon meringue, and cold, cold wine.

Go there. That's all.

There is one more feature that marks Keld Lodge out as a special place to stay: at the end of the corridor, the best drying room we've encountered, ensuring we will start the next day with dry clothes.

Ha, very ha....

Chapter 16: Groundhog Day, Keld – Kirkby Stephen

I'm beginning to regret being so sniffy about that dreary account of the Coast to Coast which turned into a book-length whinge about the fact that it rained every dammed day.

For much as it pains me to say it, we too wake to more rain, the thunder of the swollen river through Swaledale, and the knowledge that ahead of us lie the soaking, oozing, crumbling, confusing miles of a watershed crossing. This is not going to be easy.

I've already mentioned this habit we seem to have of reaching the watershed at the very moment our own lives seem most bogged down. There's almost a perverse satisfaction in seeing the landscape reflect so perfectly our personal circumstances: the boggy peat sucking at our boots, making it so much effort to take even a single step forward; literally wading through mud; the cloud sinking so low we lose not only our vision but any sense of where we are.

We've arrived at the watershed once more with a whole lot of new baggage: the stress of being a part of the sandwich generation, caring for our mum and now our uncle too, while our adult children are still very much in our lives and needing us there.

There's other classic midlife stuff too: work, relationships, money, health. More things to worry about and ask ourselves soul-searching questions about than there are weather warnings on our route.

So far, so deja vue.

The climax of a walk across the watershed is reaching Nine Standards Rigg, a collection of giant stone cairns, whose roots are a mystery, on the plateau above Kirkby Stephen.

The real mystery for us, however, is exactly the same we've

encountered on our previous crossings: whether we'll ever see what Wainwright promises to be the 'most extensive panorama' on the Coast to Coast walk, from the Lakeland skyline and Eden Valley across Swaledale out towards the Yorkshire moors.

Twice we've failed to see anything beyond the drips on the end of each other's pink noses.

First cross your stream

It might be a re-run of the previous day. We fasten the unflattering jacket hoods, dip our heads and trudge along field edges as the rain soaks our clothes. The path strikes out at right angles from the dale road, towards Ravenseat via the dramatic ravine of Boggle Hole, whose waters, a long way below, are thick and foamy.

On any other day this would be worth a coffee stop and photo. Today I think we are both too wary of the challenges we know lie ahead to pay much attention to even beautifully savage distractions such as this thunderous gorge.

There is not much more to Ravenseat itself than a silent farm which, disconcertingly given its remoteness, has a sign making it clear that on some days it's possible to take tea there.

I doubt we'd have paused even if it had been open, but it isn't – though there is a kind note saying passers-by are still 'welcome to use the facilities'.

Shushie and I have other things on our minds, primarily Whitsundale Beck which seems to be making a bid to move from beck status into the big river league.

The narrow ford we've been promised, at the gateway to the serious stage of the crossing, is the width of the road and the depth of an ornamental pond. If there are stepping stones at the ford, they are hidden by the racing, churning waters.

"You check that way, I'll try this," I suggest to Shushie, and we strike off separately in search of a place where the banks might be close enough for us to jump the swollen beck.

"Anything?" Shushie calls out after five minutes pushing through the undergrowth upstream from the ford.

"Not a hope. Stay there, I'll come to you."

I join her on the edge of the beck, 50 metres or so up from the ford and we stand together in silence for a moment, contemplating the torrent.

Eventually I say, "There's no way round. We'll have to go through. Not much point taking our boots off either. They're already soaked."

I go first, hurling my backpack across the water as seriously if I were throwing a lifeline. One slip and my worldy goods will be racing off to the North Sea. I follow, but there's no question of jumping the water. Rather, it's a plunge down into the beck, whose waters reach my waist. I have to brace against the water's force, which is certainly strong enough to push me over if not for the walking stick I'm wedging into the river bed as I inch across.

Shushie follows, remembering, I imagine, how big a disaster we'd considered her falling into the river way back in Maybeck woods.

Several months on, our decision not to worry about getting wet is precisely the about-face needed to transform this day's walking. Instead of a battle with the elements – trying to stay dry, hating the rain and mist, fearful of our own limitations when it comes to navigating a safe crossing – it feels as if throwing ourselves into the beck has somehow freed us up to treat the day as an adventure.

We're soaked. The weather can do no worse. This might even be fun.

Hags, groughs and brogs

And so it proves, despite the fact that the watershed is the wettest and craggiest we've yet encountered it.

I should explain here that it is not only the unscheduled stream crossings, the fact that there are pools and becks where there is supposed to be path, that make this route so challenging.

It is also the nature of the earth that presents a major obstacle to making progress. Wind, weather – and probably walkers – have eroded the peat so the surface is a series of teetering cliffs and hollows, scoops and drifts.

The only way through is to try and follow the dips and hollows, which means you are forever being carried away from your route. And each time you descend into them, crumbling peat cliffs rising above head height, your sense of where you are takes another hit. It is the most disorienting kind of walking I know.

Wainwright calls them peat hags (a reference whose relevance to our current state is not lost on Shushie and I), while our own guide book refers to them as groughs (pronounced gruffs I imagine). But before we came across these terms we'd decided they should be known as brogs.

Take your pick: all three names give the correct sense of a landscape that belongs on a filmset, with a life and dramas of its own.

On this occasion however, we have drawn its sting, and instead of lamenting our bad luck, we splodge and shriek our way from brog to brog, competing to see whose legs descend deeper into each beck; which of us grows the tallest from the sludge impacted beneath our boots.

It is, in a word, a triumph.

A new standard

To cap it all, as we reach the top of yet another ridge of brog we can see the distinct line of the nine standards. Not hidden in the mist-rain or low cloud but standing sentry, as perhaps they were once intended to do, signalling to the view in every direction.

It is one-o-clock. We have safely navigated the worst the watershed can throw at us and, for the first time this day, there are other walkers: a trio on a circular route, who tell us we're only the second group they've seen all day. The first were a pair of women setting out from Kirkby Stephen at nine that morning, on the Coast to Coast, which surprised us a little as we've passed no-one.

Our curiosity is only momentary for we have things to do, approaching the cairns and taking photos in every direction to memorialise this first for us: the first time we've had a view east, west, north and south from Nine Standards Rigg.

The most fanciful theory about how these pillars came to be here has primitive local tribes erecting them to try and fool the Scots into thinking the spot was guarded by an army encampment. Clearly the advocates of this particular story credit the Scots with having the eyesight of a hawk – the Scottish border is 60-plus miles away- and the intelligence of something you might find at the bottom of a bog.

Most likely the pillars were county boundaries, sitting as they do where the border between Westmorland and the North Riding of Yorkshire once ran. Alternatively, they are alerts, just like the words on those old maps: here be dragons.

Here be brogs.

Home straight

Photos taken, Shushie and I hunker into the side of one of the largest of the cairns, a little protected from the wind, happy to trade complete protection from the elements for the fantastic view.

"Hello." As we munch on flapjacks two middle aged faces peer round the side of the cairn.

"Hi! How are you?"

"Looking for somewhere to shelter actually. It's freezing up here."

Shushie nods northwards where some enterprising soul has dug a small pit for walkers to escape the worst of the weather. "There's a shelter over there if you want to get out of the wind. Where are you heading?"

"Keld." The two women have yet to break a smile.

"Coast to Coast?" I enquire.

"Mmm. It's our first day actually. We stupidly decided we only had time to do half of it so we're starting from Kirkby Stephen."

"What a day to choose to start. How have you found it?"

"Wet. What's it like ahead?"

My mind calculates. Those other walkers mentioned two women leaving Kirkby Stephen at nine. These must be them - which means it has taken them four long hours to walk the four miles up to Nine Standards. Possibly the four easiest miles of the day's walking in that there is no doubting which way to go.

I look at their despondent faces.

"It's *really* wet ahead. And hard to find the way. You might find it easier to head down and go on the dales road to Keld."

Perhaps our advice will rob them of the chance to have a real Coast to Coast experience, but I'd like to think it is the thing that will prevent them giving up on the whole walk after a single day.

Soggy but not damp

And no, there is no let-up in wetness as we walk the same four miles that they've come, except we're going downhill.

Even the bridges supposed to get us over the water are flooded.

There are distractions: the huge quarry at Hartley Fell and a field of llamas, a fascinating sky of cloud, rain and sunshine, and the prospect of afternoon tea when we reach the town.

But of course you already know from me that Kirkby promises more than it delivers. The teashop we settle our damp bodies into is as ordinary as a day in the office: a teacake made soggy by the application of watery margarine, and half cooked cheese in the bacon and brie baguette.

It doesn't matter. On this day, celebrating our first pleasurable crossing of the watershed, the one thing that can't be dampened is our spirit.

We've learned some more valuable lessons from this brilliant Coast to Coast walk:

When life throws you brogs, roll up your trousers, wade in, laugh as much as you're able, and keep going. The worst that can happen is you get soggy.

And somewhere ahead your reward will be a new view…and the divine chance to get warm and dry.

Chapter 17: Chasing eagles

For the last few weeks the soundtrack of my journeys to work has been a CD of bird sounds given to me by Shushie. She has the same CD, the idea being that if we play it enough times we'll be able to tell our blackbirds from our blue tits.

I'm dubious, given I've reached an age where I can't even rely on being able to identify the *people* I meet in the street.

But there's no doubt walking the Coast to Coast has turned Shushie and I into a pair of (admittedly poor) twitchers and wildlife watchers. We have the *I-Spy book* to prove it.

Where eagles dare

Imagine our excitement then, on our second Coast to Coast crossing, to have had an early morning encounter with England's only Golden Eagle at Haweswater.

Once upon a time Haweswater was home to a pair of eagles, blown by the winds into this rugged fringe of Lakeland, nesting high up on the rockface far from the few paths which follow the valley floor.

And then, one spring, there was only one Golden Eagle; the male remained, partnerless and perhaps with less reason to spread his wings and soar above the deep blue water.

In 2013 the RSPB has an outpost with telescope for those of us who keep returning in the hope of seeing another flying display. The more elusive the solitary eagle, the more significant we've come to feel a sighting would be – nothing less than a blessing from the natural world.

Signs

If you've never said the words 'it's a sign' then turn away now. Me, I look for them everywhere. Don't get the job/house/item on ebay? It's a sign there's something even better on its way. Walk through a glass door? It's a sign I can't see what's in front of me.

Steve Farmer's book *Animal Spirit Guides* has some words on eagles, in fact they come pretty high in Farmer's list of creatures you might want showing up in your life. He says they're a sign of new beginnings after challenging times which have taught you stamina and resilience; a reminder to rise above the mundane and focus on a greater vision for your life.

All very pertinent for us when we first saw the eagle, and no doubt why Shushie and I continue to look for the same sign all over again, returning to Haweswater to scan the fell tops for the merest hint of a golden wing.

Our golden ticket to the future?

Consolation prize

No surprise then that our next weekend leg begins with a late afternoon drive to digs at Tebay where we simply dump our bags, jump back in the car, and head for Haweswater.

The lake is as beautifully secretive as ever in the edgy dusk light. But the only things flying are annoying clouds of midges, forcing us to batten down the jackets.

Are we disappointed by the no-show? No, because our inner David Attenboroughs are about to be totally thrilled by the appearance of some chattering red squirrels at the Haweswater Hotel where we stop for a consolation cold glass of wine.

(Shame they didn't arrive sooner. According to Steve Farmer, seeing a squirrel is a sign to be extra cautious to avoid any threatening situations. Ah yes, the midges. Pink bites are now popping up from Shushie's skin faster than holidaymakers at the bar during happy hour.)

Seeing is believing

Indulge me for a moment by letting me fast-forward us to the end of the next day and our arrival in Orton after 14 miles en route.

This time it is cold beer rather than cold wine to toast the end of a beautiful day. And that is AFTER a visit to Orton's chocolate factory.

You'd think it couldn't get any better, yet as we sit and sip we spot a huge bird hundreds of metres above us, effortlessly riding the breeze. It's larger than any feathered thing we've ever seen, and certainly not one of the kites and buzzards we've learned to identify.

We watch and wonder through binoculars for a good while before the bird glides out of sight - only to return as we head into the Lakes to that night's pub b&b.

"Stop the car", I screech to Shushie. "It's there again."

We squeeze the car into the hedge and grab the binoculars. In the warm late sunshine we imagine we see a hooked beak, and gloss of shining feathers. Could it be?

I can't tell you that. Later we quiz the locals at the pub and scan the internet for any evidence that the golden eagle might venture from the shelter of Haweswater. Eagles' territories are huge, but it seems no-one has ever seen or heard of the eagle away from the lake.

But does it actually matter? We think we've been blessed by an eagle, and during those magical moments that's enough. We've been scouring the sky for a sign and there it is, come to remind us that every moment can be a new beginning and the best way of dealing with our current challenges is to rise above them, keeping our eyes firmly on a bigger vision for our lives.

Chapter 18: Stories in the stones, Kirkby Stephen – Orton

If the Vale of Mowbray is the cuckoo in the nest of the Coast to Coast – a flat interlude that doesn't fit with the majesty of the rest of the walk – then Shap is its fledgling.

It's the sort of place known only for being on the road to somewhere else. Shap styles itself a stepping stone to the Lakes but its closed-up main street suggests the majority of travellers see it as something they'd rather not step in.

On the other side of the M6, who knew Britain's only five star services at Tebay are actually named for the humble little village in their shadow?

Not us, until every bed and breakfast we try replies with a 'sorry, no vacancies' and we're forced to book into The Old School in Tebay village.

No frills

You get what you pay for, and, to be fair, at £70 for a double this is one of our cheapest stopovers.

Perfectly functional, perfectly friendly…with our room doubling up for its owners as guest bedroom and storage space. Just above our heads an artificial spruce Christmas tree overhangs the bedroom from a broad storage shelf over the shower. Talking of which, the shower itself boasts a single guest towel between us, and one of those solid buttons that you push to activate the water and then watch slide back out so the water stops. Last seen when I was five and spending Friday nights with my parents at Luton Municipal Swimming Baths.

You try shampooing your hair while also groping through soapy eyes to hit the button for water again.

The room does have a kettle, but only one mug and no teaspoon. We use our room key to fish out the teabag.

Why is it that customer service extends only to uttering the old chestnut "Let us know if you need anything" but not to explaining where the 'us' may be found.

After wandering the corridors – heavy with Saturday night cooking smells - and knocking fruitlessly on three or four closed doors, we give up.

Neither of us has the energy for a battle because back at home the last few weeks have been tougher than usual. Mum has developed a crippling breathlessness which makes it impossible for her to walk the few feet to her bathroom without hanging on to the furniture and stopping to get her breath two or three times.

The doctor says it's most likely a chest infection and prescribes antibiotics which have so far been as effective as a paper umbrella. It's a worry and we almost cancelled this trip.

Mum's health is only one reminder that there is sadness beneath the surface, despite the gloriousness of the walking. It continues with our cab driver, booked to ferry us from Orton back to the last time's end point in Kirkby Stephen.

I'm not sure why we decide to draw him out. But in the time it takes to cover the 12 miles we learn that once our driver drops us off he's heading for the florists and from there to Manchester. Manchester is where his beautiful step-daughter Carly is buried.

She'd developed stomach cancer at 18, and he takes us through the roller coaster of hopes and disappointments of their lives up until Carly died, aged 20. Though he and Carly's mum are now estranged he makes the journey to her grave once a fortnight.

Land before time

Nine standards is sunk in low cloud as usual; another reminder – this time of how lucky we'd been to finally experience it during our last leg in almost-sunshine. The watershed's moodiness is in stark contrast to the stretch from Kirkby to Orton which, on both previous occasions, has gifted us with glorious sunny days.

Not only that, but some of the loveliest views and gentlest walking of the route. The countryside from Kirkby to Orton is pure picture postcard. The rugged Yorkshire moors and lonely dales are behind; the Lakes ahead. Connecting them is an interlude of fields and streams, of quiet valleys and grazing sheep.

It may have been officially subsumed into Cumbria by civil servants, but in the hearts of those who live here, Westmorland is alive, well, and as true a window on this land's past as its ancient name suggests.

From Kirkby as far as the M6 there are unexplained mounds and barrows and dips with names that belong to legend: pillow mounds; giants' graves; the severals; and even – because you can't keep a good archer down – Robin Hood's Grave.

Wainwright remarks that at ground level there is little to see *'at least to inexpert eyes: indeed a man with other matters on his mind could walk across the site without noticing any features out of the ordinary'*.

Yet these relics of early settlements are regarded by archaeologists as some of the most important in the UK.

Perhaps their survival into the 21st century is due to the fact that they *are* invisible to most of us.

Even Shushie and I have at least half an eye beyond the stone walls where, on the horizon, the sharp dark lines of the Lake District rise and call to us.

Great walls

From Kirkby Stephen we strike out on public footpaths via the first ancient relic at Croglin Castle, and into limestone fields where startled hares and rabbits dart away.

Through a farmyard and under the Carlisle to Settle railway the route opens up into broader fields, studded with limestone outcrops like lines of teeth, and the remains of two limekilns.

We stop several times, first to greet two walkers from the other direction. "Where have you come from?" Shushie asks.

"We stayed at Newbiggin on Lune. Thought we'd go to Kirkby Stephen for coffee, then it's on to Keld."

"Good luck with that," Shushie says pointedly, though whether she's referring to the absence of decent coffee stops in Kirkby or the crossing of the watershed that follows is unclear.

Next we stop to fuss a field of Shetland ponies who turn their adorable mud-caked noses up at the only thing we have to offer – a single mushy banana.

And then to admire the dry stone-walling around these over-size fields, ingeniously put together by craftsmen who these walls have outlived many times over. A hint: if you want to be remembered build a wall. You can see the Great Wall of China from space remember?

Smardale

For a brief interlude the bleached Westmorland fields drop into a small paradise: the gorge known as Smardale. Lush green banks enclose a footbridge over the silver river which winds away past the shelved sides of ancient quarrying towards a viaduct which somehow completes the perfection of the scene.

One of the real joys of the British landscape is how a single turn in the path can offer up something completely different: an entirely new scene. Smardale is like that and it's easy to understand, as we drop down to the bridge, why the combination of trees and water and sheltered shallow gorge offered our prehistoric ancestors everything they could possibly need.

These days we need phone signals and shops and easy access to work. Even the quarry workers and inhabitants of a semi-derelict railway cottage have moved on. Leaving Smardale to day trippers like us, who arrive, ironically, looking for an escape from the demands of technology and the modern world.

Smardale's most numerous occupants now are sheep cropping the hillsides, fat bees whose busy hum becomes the soundtrack of this leg, and a giant dragonfly, flapping its wings and filling the air with a sound like the tail of a kite.

The wisdom of walkers

I should probably also note that this particular Eden taught us two things on previous visits. Firstly, to look back as well as ahead. It shames me to say that on our first Coast to Coast we might have missed the view along the valley floor and the viaduct entirely had it not been for a walker coming from the other direction who instructed us, almost officiously, to stop and take in the view behind us.

And then, on our second visit, another passing walker, hearing we were heading for Keld, asked if we were staying with Doreen Whitehead. We hadn't been planning to but his description of her scones and dinner table were all the convincing we needed.

Always, always, take the time to look all around you. And never refuse the opportunity to pick other people's brains or ask for help. Imagine if we had missed Doreen?

An eye on the prize

Above Smardale the path runs alongside more field edges, past a reservoir to meet a lonely Westmorland road and the edge of Ravenstonedale Moor.

We stop close by the moorland road to eat the sundried tomato and feta pasta kindly provided by Marks and Spencer, conscious already that the returning sun will take no prisoners. It's August and for all the unpromising start this morning, it's now blistering hot.

Ravenstonedale Moor is notable mainly for a small unprepossessing tarn – Sunbiggin – which is never without a line of twitchers' cars glinting silver in the sunshine, and the cacophanous noise of visiting and resident birds.

It is also, according to the Visit Cumbria website, considered to be the most important site in the UK for petrifying srings with tufa formation'.

If only we had known...

As it is, we've reached that stage in the day where the magnet pulling us is not tufa formations or even rare birds but the promise of cold beer and the famous chocolate factory at day's end in Orton.

Sunbiggin itself is a charming village, which seems to comprise of little more than a couple of farms. The kind with huge well-kept farmhouses and gardens looking out over to-die-for views of the Howgill Fells. And, naturally, horses and dogs.

Just outside Orton, the route passes Gamelands Stone Circle, which has weathered the passing years better even than the stone walls. Many of its original 40 posts are still standing. Not exactly China's Great Wall, but a testament to the workmanship of the tribes who put them there.

I told you that you should go and build your own wall.

Travellers' rest

And then we are in Orton, tee-shirts plastered to our backs, faces pink from the sweaty heat, fantasising about cold water and a glass of beer so chill that small droplets of condensation will form on the glass.

The only thing that could possibly make this moment even more perfect is the proximity in Orton of Kennedy's chocolate factory, where chocolate is shaped into almost every sort of creature and message you can imagine – including a special bar for Coast to Coast walkers.

We take our celebratory Coast to Coast bar to the pub and are as close to heaven as it's possible to be on earth.

Chapter 19: Doctors and distractions, Orton – Bampton Grange

There's more than one way of walking to Coast to Coast as you may have gathered from our adventures.

The norm – if there is such a thing – is to book two or three weeks' holiday and trek from St Bees to Robin Hood's Bay in a single gulp.

Or you can take four years over it, as Shushie and I did on our first east to west crossing.

You can choose speed of course. I mentioned how we first learned of speed-king Barry when we were leaving Robin Hood's Bay. So how fitting to find a message from action man himself in my inbox one day. He wrote:

"Hi. I'm the said Barry Pincer. I've walked the coast to coast many times, mostly in 5 days and under; twice in under 4 days; and once both ways in ten and a half days. I've walked the coast to coast since 1994 up until 2006. I loved every step and though some days were 19 to 20 hours I can say I savoured every minute of every step – mostly for charity, sometimes for myself."

Based on which – and the fact that this is Shushie's and my third crossing – I fear the Coast to Coast may well be addictive.

Consider yourself warned!

Walking into trouble

After the highs of sunshine and fresh air, refreshments in Orton, and our mystery bird, the phone call brings us back to earth with a solid thump.

I hear every word of Shushie's call to her partner Pud back home because the only way we can get a signal in our delightful pub lodgings is by balancing the phone on the window frame.

"Now before I say anything you're not to think about coming home," says Pud in that way that's guaranteed to make us think precisely that.

"But I'm worried about your mum. She couldn't even stand when I went in. I'm going to take her to the walk-in tomorrow. But listen, there's nothing you can do. I want you to carry on and come home when you planned to."

Shushie is silent for a moment. "I'll call you in the morning. I don't think we can make a decision now."

The single bar of phone signal dies and we look at each other. Guilt - for coming away despite Mum being poorly - and anxiety are a toxic mix, as any carer knows, and that night's meal and the sleep that follows taste of both.

Walking blind

By the next morning there is no change and we agree with Pud we may as well finish the walking we'd planned for this weekend as we can't get back in time for the doctor's appointment he's arranged. He'll call us when there's any news.

It ought to leave us free to enjoy another brilliantly sunny August day walking the velvet limestone fields of Westmorland. But instead there is an edge to everything and we choose not to make any unnecessary stops or linger anywhere, since we've moved into that frame of mind where we need to get on and get home.

It's a huge shame because this leg has much to offer, including another lovely little discovery – the Crown and Mitre serving exceptional pub grub, wonderfully social locals, soft beds and a view over the village church.

It may look like a humble village pub but it's another of those places that knows exactly what walkers coming down from the mountains need. And the restaurant staff cope effortlessly with some of our fellow guests' last minute demands: gluten free bread, no salt in the porridge, a jug of cream on the side.

Over breakfast we quiz the American family at the next table who, it emerges, are the reason the pub landlady was on the phone last night to Mountain Rescue.

They tell us that mother is their sherpa, and having hugged husband and teenage daughters goodbye at Patterdale the previous morning, she expected them to rock up to the Crown and Mitre by teatime.

By 7pm the family had not arrived. By 8pm dusk was falling and they were still missing in action from the climb up to High Street and Kidsty Pike and down the length of Haweswater. There are few phone signals up in the mountains so it was time to alert the rescue services.

Nine-o-clock, a full 12 hours after setting out, the family trudged into the pub, exhausted and famished and very conscious how much anxiety they must have caused mother Sherpa.

It turned out the group had gone wrong at Boredale House above Patterdale and spent hours trekking in the wrong direction.

The curse of Kidsty once more, about which more anon. We'd been there and done that and knew exactly how confusing that leg is.

How not to get lost

As it turns out, the pressure we're putting on ourselves to go quickly leads us to go wrong several times on the ridge above Orton Scar, heading first down a moor road and then down a farm track before we finally make sense of the very simple directions.

It's obvious this is the right way at last when small groups of determined Coast to Coasters begin bowling towards us.

The first are more American
they set out at 8.30am and
'morning tea'. Naturally we i
Orton.

Another group grips a GPS as if i
that takes away a little of the chal.
it means to be lost in the mountain.

I hope, however, they remember to i
purples of the moorland heather ui
landscapes are wide open and we car
of Lakeland but the soft animal-like sh   ...ells.

Truly, we are on top of the world again.

Be here now

One of the fun parts of this leg are the huge boulders which stud the
limestone fields, apparently dropped from space, so off-scale are
they from everything else in this high, flat country.

What surprises us, though, is that other sections of the route are
unfamiliar – particularly a wide grass track that was once a Roman
road and now belongs to sheep, grazing beneath puffs of seeds,
drifting from the trees like snow. Certainly these walks are teaching
us to notice more.

Weather talk

Hardendale is not just a pretty village hidden behind a wall, but also
the name of a quarry, and as the Roman road heads off our path leads
onto a stark white service road to the quarry.

In the near distance the M6 cuts an equally intrusive impression
across the countryside and already the noise of traffic is drowning
the sounds of birds and breeze.

we reach the steps crossing the quarry
rican friends from this morning, politely
saying how much they prefer overcast weather

cans talk about the weather too, we wonder, or is it just a
our national obsession that they choose to talk to us about the
at rather than the route…or the fact that today, so far, they are
definitely not lost.

Tea, toilets and Tebay

We have another road to cross – the M6 – via a metal footbridge
which I suspect may be used only by Coast to Coasters, for who else
would go out of their way to visit Shap. From the bridge it is the
belching chimneys of an ugly granite works which dominate the
skyline – yet it is this – plus the straggle of Coast to Coasters – which
offer Shap its only lifelines.

In a way, the village has much in common with the ancient
settlements we passed: for time has forgotten it too. Once upon a
time Shap was a key staging post and watering hole on the main road
to Scotland; its' raison d'etre demolished in moments when the M6
opened, allowing traffic to bypass its one main street.

To add insult to injury, someone built the UK's best service area at
Tebay and now no-one needs to visit Shap even for tea and toilets.

'Generally unattractive', says Wainwright dismissively, and we do
feel rather sorry for it; but not sorry enough to linger longer than it
takes to raid the cold drinks cabinet in the Co-op for something to
replace the pints of fluid we've sweated into our clothes and
backpacks.

In a weekend of pleasures, the joy of a cold drink on a scorching day
is right up there with views of the Lake District and a soft bed at the
Crown and Mitre.

120

Clots

Our next target is Shap Abbey and from there, via country lanes, we leave the official route to head back to Bampton Grange and Shushie's car.

Though only a tower remains of the Abbey, its setting in a wooded valley alongside the sparkling River Lowther gives it beauty and stature. It is easy to imagine a life of contemplation in such a perfect location.

Unfortunately, contemplation and mobile phones are not great bedfellows. Our last two hours walking are interrupted by Pud phoning from the doctors to say they're still convinced mum's mysterious breathlessness is caused by a chest infection and have doled out yet stronger antibiotics.

We try to walk off our disquiet but it's clear from the fact that we are walking ever more quickly that it's time to stop pretending our thoughts are not elsewhere.

At home the next day we call the ambulance and, four anxious weeks after mum first became breathless and unable to walk, the hospital agrees there's no chest infection. Mum's had a DVT that has moved up into her lungs and formed into several pulmonary embolisms, blocking her breathing passages and threatening her life.

I guess Shushie and I are her sherpas.

Chapter 20: The kindness of Kidsty, Bampton Grange – Patterdale

So, the curse of Kidsty.

Why cursed? Because in a landscape full of potential hazards, Kidsty Pike resembles a shark's fin and needs to be treated with the same wary respect.

The first time Shushie and I walked the path up Kidsty Howes en route from Shap to Patterdale the sun went out like a blown lightbulb the moment we began our ascent. By the time we reached the ridge, visibility was down to a few metres. Nowhere near enough to be certain of what lay either side of the path. But enough to conjure fear that the spike of Kidsty Pike itself signalled a deadly drop to the valley floor a thousand metres below.

Wind and wuthering

Wholly disoriented, and still foolish novices with maps, we did what novices tend to do and chose the path that looked safest – actually 180 degrees off our true course. We were scared and chilled to the bone and would have continued our, possibly, suicidal walk, deeper into the mountains, had we not had the good fortune to bump into the only other walkers we'd seen that day – who corrected us, spun us around and were responsible for the fact that we did, eventually, reach Patterdale.

Visit two, on our return Coast to Coast, was in some ways even hairier. As we slogged up from Patterdale everyone else was heading down, forced back by the weather they said. They warned us to do the same.

We ummed and aahed but felt we had no option, so carried on

towards the Pike where the rain turned to shards of ice and a sudden gust of wind lifted me off my feet. Fortunately it deposited me *into* the mountain.

Until that moment I had never believed it was possible to be literally blown off your feet.

It felt impossibly dangerous to continue so Shushie pulled out a space blanket and we huddled together behind a rock, debating how long we could sit it out before the freezing mountaintop temperature lulled us into a stupor of hypothermia.

I don't know how long we sat there. But once again we were lucky. For a brief few minutes the hail eased, a watery sun broke the dense cloud and we could see just enough to locate the path on Kidsty Howes and from there down to Haweswater. Drenched. Frozen. And very, very humbled, but alive to tell the tale.

Wet, wet, wet

No wonder, then, that we emerge once more from the Crown and Mitre into a soggy grey day with a lot more trepidation than excitement. Will the curse of Kidsty strike again? There is little, as we make our way along Haweswater, to suggest this time will be any different. It's raining of course and the rich, burnished ochres and reds of the Lake District in autumn are muted by mizzle. We can't see from one end of the reservoir to the other.

A word about Haweswater, since it's one of Wainwright's most anguished themes, the sacrilege that was done to the tiny village of Mardale when the valley was flooded and dammed to provide drinking water for Manchester. In times of drought it's said people flock to Hawewater, as they might to a disaster scene, curious to see what relics of that old way of life may appear briefly above the lake's surface.

Listen to the dear old curmudgeon and you'll get a skewed view of what is still, for us, one of Lakeland's loveliest spots.

Wainwright says: *"Only those who are getting on in years will remember Mardale as a charming and secluded valley...and can bring to mind the natural beaches...that are now sterile shores, arid and lifeless, sometimes beneath the water, sometimes not; or the farms and drystone walls that were engulfed and today are revealed as skeletons in times of drought...they mourn its passing for Mardale then was lovely."*

Perhaps it was, but in a different way it still is, the lonely mountains reflected in the dark lake, veins of white water tumbling down the valley sides, and a golden eagle claiming it all for his own.

Well, not quite his own for as we pass through a gigantic deer gate the damp silence is broken by a barking sound. We stop and look behind. Against the grey skyline, the outline of a stag and with him two hinds and a fawn. At our exclamation the stag springs for the cover of tall bracken, but the hinds remain, silhouetted and alert, watching us watching them. It's a magical moment.

It is four flattish miles along the edge of Haweswater to the foot of Kidsty Howes and for most of it we're forced to study our feet as we scramble for decent footholds on shiny wet rock.

Finally, opposite the crags where the eagle and his neighbours, a colony of peregrines, live, the route begins a punishingly steep ascent towards the Pike.

The only way is up

Naturally, it's cloaked in thick, murky cloud. And, equally naturally, Shushie and I are jittery. "Let's walk next to each other," she says, and there is no need for her to explain why she feels the need for close company.

As we push upwards we distract ourselves with the smallest talk we can dream up, talking about ball dresses and past boyfriends and other trivia to avoid leaving an inch of space in our minds for thoughts of fear and falling from mountains. I doubt Chris Bonnington or Sir Edmund Hillary had need of such tricks but for amateur climbers like us I thoroughly recommend it.

The climbing goes on and on: Kidsty Howes, like so many mountains and ridges, suffers from FSS – false summit syndrome. Every time you think perhaps you have reached the top and can begin to breathe again, a few more steps reveals there is yet another summit ahead.

On both sides of the path the lack of vision is unnerving. Whatever lies to the side of the path is probably not good news, and the rain seems to be getting heavier the higher we get.

But then, joy: the fuzzy shapes of two people coming towards us. There is nothing like a cloud-cloaked mountain top to remind you of your human frailty and nothing like meeting other people in such circumstances to give you a boost.

As we get closer we can see they are hunched over a map – as we have been so many times, and always on this particular peak.

"Excuse me, I wonder if you'd mind telling us where you've come from?" They are a couple, in their 30s probably, and it's the woman who speaks. Men don't ask for directions, remember.

"Bampton," Shushie tells them.

"Oh thank God! We weren't sure we were even right. It's impossible to see anything in this. We were about to give up and crack open the gin."

"Just carry on this path. It's pretty clear and if you stick to it it'll take you down to Haweswater."

"Thank you, thank you. You've no idea how you've made our day."

"I rather think we do," I mumble to Shushie as we say our goodbyes and they head off into the cloud. "That was obviously our pay it forward moment."

"That," Shushie announced, "is going to be one of today's best moments. Imagine, us being the ones to put other people right. Maybe we're getting better at this than we thought."

I can see clearly now the rain has gone

That meeting is, without doubt, a turning point in the day, and from then on there's a definite lightness to our spirits and a certainty to our steps.

We don't see Kidsty Pike, though we pass within a whisker of it, and we barely make out the Straits of Riggindale (which really sound – and possibly even look – as if they belong on the pages of *Lord of the Rings*).

But as the path rounds the Knott, a fat green mound of mountaintop, there is a cloudbreak. All around us the fells appear, stretching to Ullswater snaking in the distance, as if a magician has whipped away the black cloth covering a bowl of delights.

Such moments are always a gift. But to receive such gifts on top of Lakeland, when everything around is soft green and brown velvet, preparing for winter's sleep, is breathtaking. We've felt the fear, done it anyway, and here is our reward: a view of pure autumn enchantment.

Unbelievably, it gets even better. Up there with the Gods we suddenly hear the sharp sound of a horn and there, ahead, a pack of hounds come streaming across the felltops, beside themselves with joy at being exercised in such a lofty spot.

For full half an hour the horn continues its call, directing the pack's progress in black, brown and white waves from felltop to felltop, up and down and round-about. In their element and wholly oblivious to the watching walkers and wary sheep as they stretch out towards each summit for the sheer love of it.

Perversely, after welcoming company on Kidsty, we now find ourselves a little put out by the number of Saturday afternoon walkers emerging onto the fellsides from the Patterdale direction.

Why shouldn't they be out on the fells, with their light day packs, their noisy conversation and, in one case, their wholly unsuitable skinny white jeans and pumps? I fear a little bit of Wainwright dust may be rubbing off on us.

We stop to eat our sandwiches at the lovely Angle Tarn, from where it is a straightforward path down, via the remains of a chapel at Boredale Hause, along the valley side towards Ullswater and journey's end at Patterdale. That's when the rain starts again, ensuring we arrive at that night's accommodation at Grisedale Lodge like the two drowned rats who began the day.

Our fault, of course, for mis-timing this walk so that we have reached one of Britain's most notoriously wet regions at the most reliably damp time of year.

Still, Kidsty has been kind, and our hosts at Grisedale Lodge equally so, delivering a plate of homemade biscuits, hot drinks, hot showers, soft towels and an even softer bed.

Light and shade. Peaks and troughs. Highs and lows. In truth, one can't exist without the other and it's coming through the shade and troughs that makes the light on the high peaks so much sweeter.

We wouldn't have admitted it, but sub-consciously I think we both felt the perfection of those minutes above Ullswater were our reward for pushing through our fear of Kidsty.

Chapter 21: Wading after Wainwright, Patterdale – Grasmere

On Sunday morning our hosts at Grisedale Lodge kindly leave out the day's forecast.

It is not good.

Actually, 'not good' doesn't come close to what's predicted: torrential rain, storm winds and zero visibility.

Only a fool would venture out in this.

Well, two fools. For deluge or no, Shushie and I have no intention of not walking. These walking escapes are so precious we could no more be in the Lakes and not walk than we could take a bath without getting wet.

(Which turns out to be a rather fitting analogy, since total immersion is to be the day's theme.)

Out of the frying pan

But let me not get ahead of myself for the day has a few gifts up its sleeve to sweeten the shock of what is to come.

First, the type of Lakeland breakfast that marks the stay out as truly memorable: plates piled high with thick, lean bacon, homemade preserves and home-baked bread. Nor is our host Christine going to permit us to head out into the storm hungry, packing up doorstep peanut butter sandwiches on more of that just-cooked bread, together with homemade flapjacks.

As she serves us Chris explains how she'd initially come to the Lakes from Leeds with a job working for the Environment Agency.

Once she and husband John realised how much they loved being in the Lakes they switched to running the village shop, and finally to bed and breakfast. Yet unlike other hosts we've spoken to, both seem to have managed things well enough to ensure there remains more to their lives than bacon and clean bedding.

For instance, Christine tells us how, on a scorching day in July, they'd no guests and decided late afternoon to head up to Angle Tarn with a tent and a bottle of wine. Once they had the fells and Angle tarn's panoramic views to themselves they swam in the lake, cracked open the bottle, and dried off as they watched the setting sun turn the whole landscape to gold.

Now that, dear friends, is how to do b&b.

Our second treat comes as we begin the climb through drizzle from the Ullswater Valley floor up the side of St Sunday Crag - and remember to look behind us: the most amazing view back over the lake, surrounded by caramel hills falling towards lush green fields.

And on the other side of the valley, a flush of wild fell ponies, shyly come down to the dryer slopes while human visitors – us excepted – are still hunkered indoors.

A new route

On both previous Coast to Coast crossings Shushie and I were unable to resist the challenge of one of the UK's highest peaks – Helvellyn – and one of its deadliest ridges – Striding Edge.

Let me tell you that had we chosen to do the Striding Edge route on this occasion the day's walking could not have gone ahead. On a good day with clear visibility and not much wind, Striding Edge is still capable of claiming the unfit, unwary or simply unlucky.

Just a week before we set out we'd read of another death on the ridge. Twice we'd been lucky. Twice we had traversed it with no greater damage than racing hearts. News of this death clinched it for us; if there was something to prove then we'd proved it and had no need to ever return to Striding Edge's sharp, erratic and wholly unforgiving teeth.

Wainwright offers St Sunday Crag as an alternative, not only because it avoids the press of the ever-popular Helvellyn, but for its connection to one of his favourite walks, the Fairfield Horseshoe – one of our favourites too.

Comprising a series of gentle ups and downs and a long plateau section, St Sunday offers views over towards to the southern fells as well as the northern and western.

Let me qualify that. On one of those rare perfect Lakeland days it offers wonderful views.

As Shushie and I climb higher up the stony path out of Patterdale we can clearly see that what it is offering us is thick, lowering cloud. There is no Crag to be seen in St Sunday, much less a horseshoe.

Each step is bringing use closer and closer to the dense nothingness of walking through cloud.

Raining on our parade

Across the valley we can see the path up towards Striding Edge but not a soul on it as it too vanishes into cloud.

I feel nervous as we draw ever closer to the greyness, knowing that when we reach it our map-reading skills will be properly tested.

And that should they be found wanting, we could easily end up in another valley, on another peak, or, worse, tumbling to the valley floor.

What heightens my fear is the rain, which has now started to get serious and is coming at us horizontally, sharp and stinging, pelting our jackets and trousers so that we're forced to walk with our heads bowed to the ground.

There's no question of checking the map out in such conditions. It will be pulp in a few moments.

The only thing to do is keep putting one increasingly soggy foot in front of another and trusting with all our hearts that the path will remain clear. We know we have two miles of this assault in order to reach Deepdale Hause: the col where we will be able to descend into the head of the Grisedale Valley, just below Dollywagon Pike from where we will head up and over into Grasmere.

I am far from convinced that in these conditions, with our heads forced relentlessly to the ground, we will even notice this crucial path down. The one blessing is that beneath our feet the path had been made up with gravel, which gives the now shiny soles of our boots something to grip on.

Above the boots, everything we're wearing has now reached that level of wetness where we resemble sea creatures rather than ramblers.

Fish out of water

Fish, of course, navigate without sight and that is what we have to do.

The wind is howling around our ears making it hard to hear each other as we trudge on, growing ever colder and wetter.

I suppose there is a level of soddenness from which it is impossible to get any wetter. At this point in the day it feels to both of us as if we've reached it. Like fields flooded after weeks of rain, there is literally nothing dry left to absorb the deluge so it simply runs in rivulets from the ends of our hair, the tips of our noses, the cuffs on our jackets and the fabric of our trousers.

No wonder that I begin to get disorientated.

To avoid a steep climb up yet another of the Crag's seemingly endless mini peaks, we keep instead to the slightly lower ground to one side and emerge onto a section of flat greyness from which point there seemed to be no onward path.

Disconcertingly, given how well made the path has been all morning, the only way ahead seems to be on grass.

Which is where I now trudge, unwilling to stop for even a moment because to do so will be to allow the wind chill and sodden clothes to penetrate further a body that is already frozen to the core.

It's only continuing to move that allows me to continue to move, if you see what I mean.

Dimly, through the screeching wind and driving rain I'm aware of Shushie shouting. "Jing, Jing, where are you going?"

I swear under my breath, cross with Shushie for stopping me. I know we need to keep moving. "On towards the Hause."

"You're going the wrong way."

"How can I be? This is where we're heading."

No, you're going back the way we've come from."

It is a recognised truth that in all our walking I am the one who leads the way, who reads the map and the landmarks, and my little sister Shushie is the one who follows on.

This uncharacteristic assertiveness is not how it works. I have no choice but to stop and face into the rain to look hard at her.

She, however, is uncompromising: "Jing I promise you. I need you to trust me on this. You must trust me because for once I am right. You have turned full circle and are heading in the opposite direction to where we are going.

"You need to follow me now."

I still don't know how I could have turned full circle on the mountain top and not realised it. Nor why on that day Shushie was paying such attention to our route.

But what I can tell you is how utterly unnerving it is to discover that you can be 100% wrong about direction and about where you are and what you need to do.

Had Shushie followed me, had she not been so convinced that she was right, who knows where we would have ended up.

A bit of perspective here: I don't believe we would have died of hypothermia up on St Sunday Crag, or plunged to our deaths because I had become so wholly disoriented by the wild weather.

But it does unsettle me to realise that on another day, on another fell, had I got it so totally wrong as I did that day, those things could have happened.

Back to another important lesson of our walking the years. Ignorance and the belief that you're not the sort of person these things happen to will only get you so far in the mountains – until the day your luck runs out.

Shushie and I have, over time, developed a deep respect for what the fells demand, and what they are capable of.

More lost soles

Forgive the silly pun, and continue with us along the ridge in the white-out where the confusion over our route has made me even more nervous.

"I know yesterday we wanted the mountains to ourselves. Today I would love to see some more walkers," I shudder to Shushie.

Less than a minute later two black shapes loom out of the cloud, now so thick that they are mere feet from us when we spot them, stationary, and poring over a map.

Theirs, of course, is in a plastic envelope but much good it does them, for the rain had smeared the cover to translucency.

We reach the pair and see they are in their 30s probably, and far better equipped than us in rain-proofs, solid boots and hats pulled down tight over their ears. And yet, amazingly, it turns out they are not experts, about to put us right, but two very wet, very lost and slightly scared walkers looking for the Fairfield Horseshoe.

A little nervously the one with the beard pearled with raindrops clears his throat and says "I don't suppose you can show us where on the map we are could you?"

The effect of this simple question is like an electric jolt to our self-esteem: we clearly look as if we know what we're doing. Even more miraculously, we actually do and are able to point out that they aren't even on their own route map any more.

"Here," I say, pulling our own dog-eared and soggy map from where it nestles next to my skin beneath three layers of wet clothing. "You've come down onto St Sunday Crag. Around about here. There's your path," I point to a thin dotted line.

"Shit. We're going to have to turn round. And we came down some horrible scree to get here. Don't fancy doing that in reverse," the other walker says.

Reluctantly, they turn around and for a short time fall into step with us. We are all, I think, enjoying the companionship of other human beings in this folorn spot.

Then, another boost - a sign indicating we've reached Deepdale Hause, clearly visible as it snakes down to the valley head. We bid our new friends goodbye and good luck.

As we head down we are no less wet. No less fed up of the wind and rain and cloud. Yet our spirits are soaring. Almost 15 years since we started walking the Coast to Coast, we are now the experts!

Mountain sea

A few minutes later we pass another group, this time six walkers heading up onto St Sunday Crag where we have just descended. We pause long enough to warn them of the dire conditions they're heading into, but, like us, they say they can get no wetter so might just as well press on.

Rather them than us, for the path has brought us low enough for there to be visibility at last and ahead we can now see Grisedale Tarn like an inland sea, sitting in the bowl of Dollywagon Pike, its surface churned with white horses. Where the tarn ends above the rim of Grisedale Valley the narrow stream which is its usual outlet has become a raging river.

We've crossed it many times before on stepping stones, but nothing but water is visible. On the Helvellyn side of this new river an organised group of some 20 walkers appears to be stranded.

It takes us about 10 minutes to descend from the Hause, across marsh where our path is no longer visible beneath the new waterfalls coursing down the fellsides.

And 10 minutes for the walking group to realise they have only two choices from that position. To turn tail and return to Patterdale from where they've come. Or to wade through the river at the valley head.

Fascinated, and secretly smug that it is someone else's turn to go swimming on the Coast to Coast, we watch as one by one the walkers tentatively step into the water, in places up to their thighs, carefully placing sticks to prevent the current from dragging them towards the drop.

It is a walk they will no doubt always remember, and a measure of how strange the conditions are on that day.

Sadly for us, the group still beat us to the path leading around the grey ocean-like Grisedale Tarn, up and around to the head of Great

Tongue Gill, from where we will all descend to Grasmere.

I say sadly, for at this point we would happily have walked alone again. Instead, we are part of a crocodile, gingerly picking its way across slippery stones, down a narrow and treacherous trail, with frequent stream crossings to add to our saturation levels.

A last soaking

There is one, short reprieve as we descend: a break in the weather than lasts just long enough for us to haul those peanut butter doorsteps from our rucksacks, blessing the fact they're wrapped in plastic, in order to put a bit of instant fuel into our freezing bodies.

It is also long enough for the walking group to put some distance between us and them. But we don't dare linger long over this late lunch for fear we could still chill.

Oddly, we almost welcome the distraction from the cold that the challenges of the route pose. The usual path has been swallowed in an unfamiliar landscape of impromptu waterfalls and fresh streams, flowing down the slopes like trails of white seaweed.

Concentrating on finding a way around and through these we forget, for a while, how very, very cold we were.

There is one more thing that is enabling us to remain cheerful-ish as we put one squelching boot in front of the other.

Shushie's wonderful friends, Kay and Steve, who have supported every leg of our walking vicariously, volunteered to meet us in Grasmere, and taxi us back to the Crown and Mitre at Bampton where all four of us can enjoy a catch up.

Bless their generous hearts: they find us camped out in Green's tea room in Grasmere, unable to stop shivering despite the hot tea we're cupping our hands around. Beneath both chairs, cartoon-style puddles are growing ever larger as the wetness seeps from our skin and clothing, our walking sticks and boots.

It is, quite possibly, the wettest we have ever been while walking and the reason why, when we finally reached the comfort and steamy heat of our room at Bampton, the ecstatic noises emerging from the shower must have embarrassed any guests in neighbouring rooms.

After our showers we slip beneath the fat duvets with more hot tea, feeling our toes for the first time that day, as close to bliss as it is possible to be on this earth.

And there is still a large glass of wine, steak pie and chips, plus the comfort of easy talk with friends to look forward to that evening.

We'd have preferred sunshine for the walking. But warmth comes in many forms.

Good food, good friends, good fortune. Our cups are running over - just as our clothes had been a few hours earlier.

Chapter 22: Walk Interrupted

As you know our plan was to walk once a month, a weekend at a time, to complete the Coast to Coast in a year.

Then life got in the way again.

Not the life of our hillwalking, the fresh mornings and soaring fells; the skies where we never cease to look for a golden eagle's wings; the rest, and honest talk in front of a welcoming pub fire at dusk.

No, this was our lives as carers, parents and partners back home - which played such a big part in us deciding to re-walk the Coast to Coast in the first place. A reason, once a month, to ring-fence a couple of precious days for our own souls, to restore ourselves a little, and reconnect over something more than medicines, check-ups and endless, endless arrangements.

Picking up

In late October, returning south from Grasmere with a notebook full of jottings and hearts equally full of memories, another blow hits us.

Unbelievably, Shushie's father in law has also had a stroke, only unlike mum's four years earlier, Maurice's stroke robs him of virtually every faculty, including speech and the ability to move anything more than one arm.

Just a few weeks after all the worry and round trips seeing mum through treatment and recovery from pulmonary embolisms in Stoke Mandeville, Shushie's hospital duties resume.

She now has two sick parents on her books, one of them touch and go, plus a partner in Pud who needs her to be a rock for him as he's been for us all this time with mum.

Another month, another hospital

And then mum gets sick again too, this time a flare-up of the breast cancer which had seen us trugging backwards and forwards to the Royal Marsden for radiotherapy all summer long.

A week before Christmas she is given an urgent referral to see a specialist and on New Year's Eve an appointment for a mastectomy two weeks later.

Both before and ever since she has mainly retreated to the armchair, her world shrunken to the living room and tv where she more or less remains today.

Enough

There have been other awful family challenges, too personal and uncertain to write about here, but, together, simply too much and too raw for us to walk away from. By November we are clear there will be no more walking in 2013, and our ambition to complete the Coast to Coast within a year has to be let go; as so much has had to be let go of even while we walked.

Feeling the fear

There is more to those months away from the fells too.

Another fear has accompanied us for much of the Coast to Coast route so far, but one that mostly went unexpressed.

It is the fear Shushie and I share in quiet moments that the years of caring, of living with heads that are never free from the insidious soundtrack of doubt, anxiety, guilt and overwhelm, are ageing us, far more than simple biology.

That middle age is passing by and the things we promised ourselves, all the living we have yet to do, will be stolen away by the reality of having got lost in the relentless business of trying to manage other people's lives.

Old lives

I recall many years ago when I was writing *The Carer's Handbook* someone I interviewed saying to me, despairing, 'I am living the life of an 80-year-old woman'. Now I know, really know, what he meant. That so much is clipped and defined by mum's capabilities and the responsibilities we've chosen to take on – even while she increasingly fails to respond; giving less and less of herself back.

For Shushie, there is as well the great sadness of her strong father-in-law being toppled and made helpless by a stroke, trying to hold up those who are holding him up.

For me, used all my life to looking out for her, the fear that my sister might get ill through stress.

More ill, I mean, for already the frozen shoulder and psoriasis are like clamps on her life force, daily reminders of being under intense strain.

I fear illness for myself too. For the last four months my shoulders have been clenched and sore, in sympathy, or because life wants me to know that I need to unburden. We both do.

I've always spoken the truth when I say to others that life goes on getting better. Now I wonder if that is still true or whether something in my spirit is ageing; something crucial to experiencing life as beautiful, joyful and endlessly rich.

So that when, eventually, the time comes that it is just us again it will be too late. We will have forgotten how to be young at heart.

I know these are not fears that are special to us, to carers, or indeed to many in their middle years, facing the loss of friends, family, the roles which defined them for two decades or more and, before that, the reassuring rules of childhood.

That's the thing about midlife: until now change has been a constant and yet also, in a way, expected. The changing scene of this period of our lives feels somehow uncharted and therefore so much more personal and profound.

Passing time challenges us to redefine who we are if we are no longer parents or employees or any of those other easy certainties; and rethink what it is we want from the years that are left.

My fear is I will start to listen to the quiet, poisonous whispers of each successive birthday, each new number, each small reminder that we no longer bounce back the way we used to.

That I will begin to believe that energy spent in one area of life is no longer available for other things. Whereas once I was certain the supply was endless.

On a fine spring day in early 2014, as Shushie and I sit in her garden, contemplating a return to our walk, we watch bees and butterflies and ladybugs emerging from a winter of hibernation.

And I pray that we might shake off the staleness of stress and find that small promise of spring in our own hearts. Not just now, for this return to the Coast to Coast. But ever after.

Chapter 23: A thousand words for rain, Grasmere - Rosthwaite

I guess the title gives it away.

After that long, long interlude, after the demands of home forced us to postpone any notion of completing our Coast to Coast walk during 2013, after the wettest winter on record, what did we expect when we resumed?

Er, more rain?

It is the first weekend of April 2014. Six long months have passed since that soggiest of crossings from Patterdale to Grasmere…and we wake in our Keswick guest house to leaden skies and that brand of driving rain that cuts the sky like sheets of steel.

If our earlier Coast to Coast crossings qualified for the slowest 190 miles on record then this little outing is certainly shaping up to be the wettest.

Still, even the drag of rain is relative when you are feeling as stir crazy as Shushie and I.

It might be hard to tell sky and ground apart, judging from the simple sogginess of *everything*. Squelching out of Grasmere, our jackets already as slickly wet as the slate roof tiles of the houses we pass. The paths might be under several inches of water.

But we are finally moving.

We are back among the mountains. And ahead lies the promise of soft fell air, the surprisingly sweet smell of wet grass and damp sheep, and the raw, wildness of the felltops.

Turn and turn about

Deposited into Grasmere by a taxi, we notice it's full of despondent weekenders, forced to abandon the hills for a morning of souvenir shopping and coffees behind steamy glass windows.

We make only one concession to the downpour. We will not tackle Helm Crag, whose rocky outline is entirely submerged in cloud. We will, instead, head up the valley of Easedale, from whose head we believe it will be easier to find our way over a landscape we nervously remember as being without much in the way of navigational features.

This is most certainly not a day for getting lost or walking a step further than necessary.

The few walkers we encounter seemed to feel the same. Initially we're passed by what I'll politely call a spritely 'seniors group' (and don't think I don't know they are probably attaching the same label to Shushie and I), and by a huddle of distinctly reluctant youngsters who, judging from their Spanish-Costa-type clothing, are not used to fellwalking.

Not long after, both groups pass us again, this time heading back to where they've come from.

We have the fells entirely to ourselves.

Well, apart from the rain that is.

Wet, wet, wet

I am going to blame the rain for the fact that there is so little to report on this leg. All of our effort goes into picking out the least worst (for which read waterlogged) of all the route options. It is too rainy to stop and certainly too wet to get my notebook out.

Mainly what we see is a landscape of hazy green, as through a sheet of cling film. Becks swollen to torrents, their thunder drowning out any other sound.

A wet tide rising up from our boots to saturate our trousers first, then our jackets, where the waterline coming in the opposite direction, down from our hoods and necks to our backs, meets it.

It is, as I said, raw. And scary and hostile and unknown. And yet also awesome in its unknownness.

Surfing the sky

If the Eskimos have 100 or more words for snow, I'm beginning to feel we need the same for rain – to prevent you experiencing deja vue as you read this. And to differentiate this day's downpour from those I've described on every other recent leg.

Perhaps the simplest way of characterising these April 'showers' is to tell you that when we do reach the top of Easedale, and the landscape opens into the common – a large scooped bowl contained by ridges to the north and west – it has turned into a shallow lake.

We set out across it, careless of the water for once again it's scarcely possible to get wetter. We hope that our sense of direction is taking us to Greenup Edge, the gateway from one valley into the next – Borrowdale. Our eyes are peeled for any hint of distinguishing landmark that will show us we're right.

From the top of Greenup we pause only long enough to admire the sheets of rain: the wind has built to a fury and the rain now ressembles huge rollers out to sea: wave after wave, tearing up the sky.

The descent into Borrowdale is down a series of stone steps slicker than a seal's skin, while the wind flings itself at our backs.

Three times I fall, wind-assisted. While beside me Shushie's cartilage makes an ominous click with every step she takes, strained need to move forward and apply our brakes at the same time.

It's as hairy as anything we've walked through so far.

Smoke signals

But eventually we're down and the path is a gentler descent, running alongside an unrecognisable Stonethwaite Beck which now half fills the valley floor, its surface as churned and frothed as an ocean storm.

To our right, the fellsides are equally unrecognisable. In place of gentle grassed slopes fat white arteries of water plunge down to soak the path.

The tops look as though they are set along their length with fires. It's actually the water, whipped into great smoking clouds of spray by the wind: smoke signals warning walkers to stay at home.

We get the message and hurry on, as fast as Shushie's clicking leg, and the new rivers swamping the path every few metres, will allow.

As we pound along, we notice how even the trees have turned to waterfalls, the rain making cloaks of water down their darkened trunks.

Where can this amount of water possibly go?

Drying out

We find a part of the answer when, after a seven hour soaking, we finally reach Rosthwaite and the bus stop to take us back to Keswick. Inside our waterproof backpacks are several inches of water swirling at the bottom. My purse swills back and forth in the water.

Sitting steamy in the bus, the water literally runs off us to create ponds around our feet.

On the plus side, we have once again lucked in with our accommodation. TripAdvisor has directed us to Sevenoaks guest house –named because it is at 7 Acorn Street – and the moment we see the rooms are named for famous mountaineers we're hooked.

The place has just been taken over by the lovely Sue and Iain Ross, who are nervous about living up to the reputation of their predecessors who were responsible for its top three TripAdvisor rating. But they need have no fear.

We are welcomed by a determination to help us dry out everything we own, by a large comfy room with mountain views, Easter chocolates on the bed and homemade biscuits on the tea tray; by the promise of pancakes, syrup and strawberries for breakfast; and by a friendliness that is the perfect tonic for yet another challenging Coast to Coast day.

If you want to try it you might get really lucky and end up staying in the Wainwright room, feeling inspired to walk the Coast to Coast too.

Er, during a dry period?

Chapter 24: The art of slowing down

The man is about our age, kitted out in a white tee-shirt and khaki shorts, and doesn't look anywhere near apologetic enough.

"I hope you're not in a hurry." His weak smile suggests the little scene playing out between his son, the gate, and our wish to pass through it, really has nothing to do with him at all. "Do you have children?"

We've been standing there a few minutes while the son, no more than 6-years old but with the lungs of a football fan whose team has scored in the last minute, plays with the gate: pretending to open it then shoving a firm little hand over the catch and screaming if his dad tries to intervene.

With his back turned to his dad, the expression directed at us is not mischief but earnest malevolence I would not have believed a six year old capable of.

Waiting for Damian

And yes, we assuredly are in a hurry. Despite the glorious blue sky overhead, the beauty of the drive through Borrowdale to get here, the green lushness of this forest path connecting Rosthwaite (where we'd left off in April) and Seatoller, the purple foxgloves and the wild garlic smells, we are desperate to get moving.

Two hours earlier we'd been up and out of our glorious guest house at Ghyll Farm in record time, stationed alongside the village school in Ennerdale Bridge waiting for a ride with Damian of Bigrigg taxis. It was pleasant at first, standing in unaccustomed sunshine, enjoying the sound of others' walking boots as small groups of Coast to Coasters starting out on only day two of their trek east, marched up the road and turned down a narrow lane towards Ennerdale itself, a vast slick of silver filling the valley floor up to the point where the fells sweep down to meet it.

The minutes passed and so do more people, including a group from Melbourne we'd met in the pub the night before, and who'd admitted day one had been tougher than expected and a taxi had been enlisted to shorten their day. The fact that there'd been four of them last night and only three of them this morning suggested it had become even tougher overnight – as it is prone to do when muscles are untested.

But we are in no position to feel superior, particularly as the minutes pass without the slightest suggestion of a taxi's diesel engine to disturb the Saturday morning peace.

Our journey up the previous day was planned around having a few hours spare to walk around Wasdale, now we are so firmly in the western Lakes – an area Shushie and I have done very little exploring in.

But we'd set out late, having had to deal with putting one of mum's cats to sleep. It would have seemed wrong to rush away at the crack of dawn when we were all quietly grieving the end of another small era.

And then the entire British population chose June 20th to head up the M6 and we crawled and sweated and cursed the electronic warning signs which we blamed for keeping us from our precious lakes.

By the time we reached junction 36 – the magical number at which you can truly believe you are in the Lakes – it was clear there'd be no time for walking but only watching and yearning through the car windows.

So Damian's no-show is merely an extension of the previous day's frustration (and, I'll be honest, there are a few tears and I did say it isn't fair after all we've been through, and if there hadn't been other walkers around I would certainly have stamped my foot).

Long story short, after we (using the public phone box for reader, it doesn't matter what your network, no signal can penetrate Ennerdale – the most westerly and remote of the Lakes), our hosts at Ghyll Farm and the landlord of the Shepherd's Arms are unable to reach Bigrigg, we jump in Shushie's car with no plan other to drive to our starting point and worry about the car being in another valley an hour's drive from our end point later.

En route to Cockermouth and the A66 Shushie suggests I see if I can raise any taxi drivers there and it is Barry of Cockermouth Taxis who rescues us from a layby on the outskirts of town and spirits us into Borrowdale, telling us, as the locals always do, that you wouldn't catch him walking the fells, but then admitting that his favourite occupation in the world is to pack a sandwich and spend the day sitting alongside Bassenthwaite Lake with a fishing rod, the birds, his thoughts and Skiddaw's magnificent shadow in front of him.

So yes, we are starting out two hours later than we'd planned with 14 miles of fellwalking ahead and we are, without question, in a hurry.

Slow time

Eventually, with no help from the boy's useless father, we are allowed to pass through the gate.

The view opens up. The path starts to climb slightly, up towards Honister, between bright green-cloaked fells while behind us lies Borrowdale like the wooded valleys of childhood fairytales.

Overhead the sky is the colour of a tropical pool, with drifts of white clouds only accentuating its blueness.

The fellsides are jewelled with buttercups and purple thistleheads and white puffs of cotton grass. The air smells of dew and promise. It is the longest day of the year and will be light until at least 10pm. Really, it couldn't be a more perfect day for a walk.

And we, who've remarked regularly during recent legs of this walk on how much longer it is taking us to let go of home and relax and just be where we are, who, in truth, sometimes haven't even managed to wholly relax at all, realise that now we're wound as tight as the compress on a broken artery. With the same sort of stifling effect on our hearts and souls.

That's why that playful six year old became, in our minds, a little terrorist, put there to defy us.

"You know what," Shushie says, "We just have to let it all go, allow ourselves to take as long as it takes to do this walk. So what if we don't get back till the evening? We're here now and it's the longest day and it's not going to rain. Let's just not worry about what time we get back, and if we miss dinner we miss it."

So we do. Slow down that is.

We let go of our shoulds and ought tos and allow the day to run its own course.

And we stop worrying.

And if you want to know the lesson in this making a choice to let go of our timetable and expectations it is that the rest of the day, and the day that came after, our final days on the Coast to Coast, are quite possibly some of the best and brightest of our lives. So far.

If we could learn every day to press those switches as successfully as we did that day then how many more best and bright days could we open our hearts and minds to?

Chapter 25: A day among the giants, Rosthwaite – Ennerdale Bridge

Turns out we aren't the only ones running late.

From Seatoller to the top of Honister, where a slate mine stands sentry at the dramatic gateway joining Borrowdale and Buttermere, is a mile and a half of uphill walking.

As we ease our way uphill, happy now to stop every hundred metres in order to turn a full 360 degrees for the view, we see only cars. No people.

It's a different story when we reach the mine, where anxious stewards in fluorescent vests are scanning the fells to the east, muttering to each other about there not being enough time. Close by a trestle table holds a few mean plastic beakers of very weak orange squash.

We are ready for refreshment and park our rucksacks and sticks close enough to be able to follow the unfolding drama. Apparently we've stumbled on a 10 in 10 event for an MS charity: ten miles in ten hours, which would be generous on flat ground, but appears to involve something like ten serious peaks today.

(For the record Shushie and I reckon on averaging two miles an hour for the Coast to Coast, the frequent uphills and our commitment to regular stopping to simply sit and look, compensating for those times on the flat when our feet are flying – er hum – at least for the first few hours of the day.)

The stragglers huffing and puffing into sight are, it emerges, almost six hours into their allotted ten, and have so far clocked up just four miles. Someone at head office has clearly never been walking in the Lakeland fells.

Clueless

To add to this rather ungenerous sense of our superiority, as Shushie takes photos, a lycra-ed cyclist heaves up to me from the steep climb we've just done.

"Is that an OS map?" his bike rams into my leg but then there's so much sweat on his face I imagine he can't see what he's doing.

"Can you show me where we are on it?"

I do of course, all the while thinking 'bloody hell, this is Honister Pass, one of the most famous intersections in the Lakes, and we are sitting outside Honister slate mine, which is on not only on every map but has a dirty great sign on it.

'How is it you can ride a mile and a half uphill in scorching sunshine without knowing where you are going?'

One thing we learn that day is that come the summer, come the crowds who don't know a compass from a cucumber sandwich. Folk who, on any other day but one such as this, with perfect conditions, panoramic views as far as the Irish Sea, and plenty of people with maps to ask, would be a huge liability to themselves.

You will know, of course, from what I've written earlier, that the only reason Shushie and I recognise this phenomenon is because that was once us - clueless on our first Coast to Coast crossing.

We are not so superior now that we don't feel a little anxious for all those coming in the opposite direction from Ennerdale clutching nothing more than a roughly photocopied sketch of their route, and no idea that the Lakeland fells would be so, well, high!

On top of the world

Talking of which, there's no let-up in the gradient after our coffee stop.

Leaving behind the school groups and coaches at Honister Slate Mine the route joins a disused – vertical – tramline, introduced to save quarry workers from the dangerous job of bringing Honister's prized green slate down from the fells on hurdles, which they had to walk in front of as human brakes on the weight.

But each upward step on slippery shale is, we know, bringing us closer to one of Lakeland's stop-in-your-tracks-and-know-there-is-a-heaven views: out towards Buttermere and its neighbour Crummock Water, nestling in the lee of Haystacks, beneath High Crag and High Stile, overlooked by Fleetwith Pike.

There is nothing to do when we reach the top but stop. And sit. And wonder at it all.

To commit it to memory, so it can bring us back aloft on all the future days when our boots are mired in mud, or grey skies threaten to overwhelm us.

Everything is in such sharp relief: every shadow cast by fluffy clouds on the soft velvet of the slopes; the dancing light and shade of the lakes below; grey rock jagging out from the summits like the teeth of a predator; narrow stone paths picking a way across the fells; in the distance, all this wildness flattening to yellow fields and beyond them the suggestion of pale sea; in front of us, across the plunging valley towards Hay Stacks, the merest glimpse of mountain lake – Innonimate Tarn where Wainwright, our guide, chose to have his ashes scattered.

Of all the fells and dales he walked, this place, this view, was where he felt he would find the most peace through eternity.

And on this day, drinking it all in as thirstily as if our veins have become desiccated during the long, long months before, we cannot argue.

Stumbling and signs

For a mile or so, the Coast to Coast route stays on top of the world, following the colourfully named Moses' Trod – an old cairned road, along which the slate was transported to Wasdale and the west coast.

But Moses was more interested in another kind of hard stuff. According to folklore he made his living from distilling and selling moonshine amongst the felltop crags. Perhaps Moses' Stumbled might have been a more accurate name for this lovely path.

Eventually it's time to leave our mountaintops via the steep descent of Loft Beck, a kind of chimney stack plunging down into the valley of Ennerdale, between rocks and gulleys so you are forced to twist your body and legs every few steps to accommodate a new angle in the gradient.

Here it is that Shushie and I encounter the same groups of walkers we saw leaving Ennerdale Bridge, only now they no longer look fresh in their new boots and shiny walking gear, but bothered and tentative. Where are they? Are they on the right route, they ask? Is there far to go? And, are they even capable of such a relentlessly demanding climb aloft?

My guess is that within two days this little group will be taking boat rides on Windermere and cream teas in Ambleside, having realised the Coast to Coast is no walk in the (national) park.

Cruelty to trees

Even at the bottom of Loft Beck we are still less than halfway through the day's allotted 14 miles.

Ennerdale Valley is only partly silver lake. Coming from the east there are some four miles of forest to march through before the shining waters of this remote silent lake are glimpsed.

It doesn't matter: we were loving every minute of the day, our bodies are working well despite recent lack of use, the sun is still shining, and now we've crossed over with the west-to-easters we have the whole lovely valley entirely to ourselves.

We speed past Black Sail Hut – claimed as the most remote youth hostel in England – our eyes constantly turning back to the great tombstones of Great Gable and then of Pillar, solid grey walls of rock rising from the valley floor to stare at the giants that can be found in the neighbouring Wasdale valley.

Into the forest proper, which once seemed to us as it seemed to Wainwright: a mutation.

You can hear his gruff Yorkshire voice in what he writes: *"Where there are now plantations of conifers there used to be fellsides open to the sky, singing birds and grazing sheep. It was Herdwick country...Those of us old enough to remember the valley as it was are saddened by the transformation. Lovers of trees paradoxically will not like the hundreds of thousands that make up Ennerdale Forest: deformed, crowded in a battery, denied light and air and natural growth. Trees ought to be objects of admiration, not pity. Trees have life, but thank goodness they have no feelings else here would be cruelty on a mammoth scale."*

Since his time, and ours too, the landscape has been altered in both negative and positive ways: a disease is killing the larch trees, their loss opening up the canopy; while the Forestry Commission, no doubt stung by the way followers of Wainwright's route have amplified his criticisms, has begun a programme of planting native species.

As we walk we can see into the forest – it's no longer an

impenetrable dark green wall – and on both sides of the path banks of wildflowers are thriving. Apart from our boots, perfectly in time with each other, the loudest sound is the buzz of bees gorging on the nectar of purple wild orchids, pink campion and daisies, while the occasional fat dragonfly feasts on the midge clouds which accompany us.

Robin Hood's again

There's the sound of our voices too.

Conscious of the approaching end of this Coast to Coast crossing we suddenly feel an urgency about all that needs to be said and resolved. To extract every single lesson we can from our odyssey.

Recalling highlights and lowlights. Musing together on what we're taking away. I'll tell you more in a moment.

We reach the lake finally, following the narrow shore path which teeters over tree roots as complex as tangled wool, spreading over and around the rocky path in search of something to fasten onto.

And as we pick our way among the rocks and roots, the scent in the air is of the sea, though that still lies some miles ahead. Perhaps it is no more than our imaginations but with white horses racing across the lakes' surface, the rich tang of weed, it is a taster of what is to come the next day.

We continue to allow ourselves to stop, despite the deepening day, stripping off boots and socks to cool our feet in the lake. And to look back towards the valley head where clouds are now mustering, darkening the fellsides. As they do so the shadows seem only to intensify the golden fingers of late afternoon sun, shining our way home, turning the lake into liquid light.

We are leaving the fierce felltops behind, but only with our bodies. Our spirits remain aloft, drunk as that man Moses on all the beauty we've seen this day; all the awe we've felt, all the peace we've found.

Ennerdale has one final challenge for us: Robin Hood's Chair, a strange rock promontory jutting out into the lake, where the path effectively disappears and the only way past is by scrambling over its top, with extreme care.

Our guide books are silent on the subject of why this obstacle, so remote from Sherwood Forest, is named for the outlaw, but as they point out, it's a neat connection between the almost start and end of the Coast to Coast walk.

Actually, there is another challenge for two walkers who, after all that road walking through the forest, fully understood the meaning of the expression 'footsore': another mile and a half on tarmac to bring us into Ennerdale Bridge, the village.

I've often noted how much longer than a mile is the final mile of any day's walking. This one goes on forever and the only thing that helps us continue to put one tired boot in front of the other is the thought of sharing a celebratory cider once we reach the village.

We've arranged to call Barry for a lift back to the car in Cockermouth and he is as good as his word, standing by to get our call and saying it will take him 20 minutes to reach us. The perfect amount of time to buy a cold, cold cider and sit with it outside The Shepherd's Arms in the sunshine, looking out towards the fells that have been with us all day, with full hearts and utter satisfaction.

Chapter 26: More walking wisdom

One of the conversations Shushie and I promised ourselves for this final weekend is a review of our original 'This much we know' list.

Remember the one about always choosing pie if it's on the pub menu and homemade?

After a run-in in Keswick with one of the ugliest pies ever to darken a pastry case you can scratch that little gem from the list and make up your own mind.

Just the same, there are a few new little morsels of learning we're happy to share with anyone thinking of following in our slow old footsteps:

A mile can be any distance

Forget what they taught you in school (1,760 yards = 1 mile for us pre-decimalisation students) one mile is definitely not the same as the next. *Every* mile towards the end of a full day's hiking is at least three miles long. Honestly. Whereas when you're up among the felltops on a glorious summer's day a mile passes in a moment. There is nothing to do about this strange phenomenon except to keep putting one foot in front of the other.

Pack a flask

Yep, it's heavy, but on a cold or wet day it's as comforting as fluffy bed socks and the roaring log fire you're dreaming of. On a sunny day it's the perfect excuse to stop and sit.

You already know this, I'm certain, but the *only* hot drinks that have a place in said flask are instant coffee and hot chocolate (preferably not at the same time). And this from a coffee snob who wouldn't touch instant at any other time.

Do NOT, under any circumstances, put tea in your flask, unless you have a taste for the contents of the u-bend beneath the kitchen sink.

Packed lunches are goody bags for grown-ups

When we were kids holidaying in Blackpool, landladies were as terrifying as the characters in a Roald Dahl book; you wouldn't dare leave anything on the plate, complain about the nasty Izal loo roll, or stay out later than the nine-o-clock news.

The option to holiday overseas, and the success of TripAdvisor, have changed all that. Which means self-respecting b&bs carry on trying to impress, even after you've packed up and paid. Fresh-baked bread, football-sized wedges of homemade Victoria sponge, fruit from the garden, hams and cheeses from the local farmer's market: the rustle of that brown paper bag they hand you holds as much promise as the most beautifully-wrapped birthday gift.

Take a 360 degree view

Ignore the song that says don't look back. Always look back and look up too. In fact look everywhere. There's a reason that after finishing our first Coast to Coast we turned around and walked back in the opposite direction: it gave us such a different perspective we might have been on a totally different walk. To (mis)quote another song: Life is all around.

Always takes the chance to paddle

Walking in wet feet is not the worst thing in the world. Trust me on this: we are the experts. Besides, which would you prefer: the sticky wetness of sweat inside hot boots, or sliding damp feet that have been cooled and soothed in a mountain beck back into those crusty socks?

Write a list of essentials and keep it with your backpack

I can't believe I'm writing this. I'm absolutely certain no-one reading this has ever driven 200 miles to go walking to discover they've forgotten to pack their boots. Actually, neither have we. But we have accidentally left behind, in ascending order of inconvenience: toothpaste, pyjamas, flask, compass, jacket, map, shoes to wear when we're not wearing boots, oh, and the actual backpack too.

We now have The List. It's just about remembering where we put it.

Lighten your load

Talking of backpacks, and their big brothers, rucksacks, unless there really is no alternative to carrying two weeks' of clobber on your shoulders, your enjoyment of the scenery, the conversation and the whole day will be in direct proportion to the size of your load.

The man we met in the woods carrying on his back everything he needed for two weeks, tent and cooking equipment included, could neither tell us where he'd been or where he was going. His whole body was set to endure rather than enjoy.

You'll excuse me for slipping into teacher mode for a moment, but I can't resist making an analogy here with one of the key lessons in the workshops I run: ditch the baggage. Get it all out; all that icky stuff that's keeping you stuck, that you're still carrying out of habit, or fear, or because it never occurred to you that without it you'll be able to move forward a whole lot faster.

Actually, while you're at it, you might also want to ditch, this time in no particular order: expectations, frantic busy-ness, stress, seeking approval, martyrdom, ignoring your own needs, over-giving, trying to 'be good'… and fighting and railing against the reality of how things are.

Chapter 27: Crisis, Chance and Choice

It's 16 months since I wrote, on the eve of beginning this Coast to Coast crossing, 'bring it on change'.

I wrote from a belief that our lives were somehow on hold, strangled into relentless routine by becoming full-on carers for the second time. I wrote from a sense of wistfulness for the other times we had walked this way: when the four years it took in each direction were accompanied by profound and *mostly positive* shifts in both our lives. As the scenery changed from sea cliff and lofty moorland, through soft dales to soaring fells, so our circumstances shifted too.

Secretly – because of course it makes no real sense – I believed that it was our walking that somehow forced the change. That each step towards west or east coast sent a signal to the universe that it needed to do its part. To reward our physical efforts by rearranging the landscape of our lives.

In the introduction to this book I quoted Sarah Ban Breathnach's words in her book *Something More*, "There are three ways to change the trajectory of our lives: crisis, chance and choice."

What this new Coast to Coast was really about, I think, was forcing our hands on those things. We'd both reached a point where it was hard to see quite how life could go on as it was. We were exhausted, lost, frustrated, and in denial about some of the nastier emotions we sometimes felt. I'd labelled the small breakdowns I was experiencing as burnout. Shushie hinted at something even darker.

Fledging

This darker side of life wasn't only about having to accommodate the caring in already busy lives, though there were days when I wanted to rail about how unfair it all was. Unfair on us, who had already spent five years in our forties caring for an uncle who had been very little to us when he was well, but so little to other people too that there seemed no-one else to take on his care.

Unfair on me, who, in the same week mum was felled by a stroke, was looking forward to the first child fledging -beginning a gap year in Australia which ought to have heralded the first small promise of freedom as an empty nester.

Most of all, unfair on our mum, one of the strongest women we knew, whose daily round of visits to sick friends, day centre, lunches, outings and quiz nights, involved walking – marching in her case – miles every day. It was inconceivable that someone so fit, so determined, so stubborn, might be stopped in her tracks when for 78 years nothing and no-one else had been able to persuade her to change course.

Please understand, I know that there is nothing special about our situation. Other people care. Some of them care more and better than we do. Other people – including mum perhaps – have much more to deal with.

But we can only be us and experience our own lives. And all of this was happening to *us* at a time when we'd been led to expect life should be opening up.

When the long, tough years of making and breaking relationships and hearts, of bringing children through their own, significant challenges, of juggling demanding jobs along with it all, and just, well, trying so damm hard day-in and day-out to get it right for everyone else, ought to have been levelling out, like the jagged peaks and deep valleys of the Lakes, melting into the gentle green cushion of the Yorkshire Dales.

We were due that.

The big 'c'

So now Shushie and I are pounding through Ennerdale Forest in sunshine, as conscious of the perfectly delicate stems of pink orchid as we are of Pillar's sharp outline towering above us like a tombstone that, even on this summer's day, remains always in shade, dark and unknown.

We are one day and no more than 20 miles from the end of a walk that has taken us half a year longer than we expected. The first 'c' – crisis: Shushie's father in law suffering a massive stroke too; mum's pulmonary embolism followed by the breast cancer becoming so aggressive she needed a mastectomy; and other even no less devastating crises involving close family and friends that wholly floored us - but are not our stories to tell.

Choosing life

"Doing this walk again saved my life," Shushie says as we soak up the sun and the scenery.

I wait; want to know that she doesn't mean she thought of ending it.

"Many times I felt myself teetering on the edge of a black hole. I don't mean I'd have stepped into it, not that. Getting seriously ill, something I wouldn't recover from, going out of my mind. It was there, waiting for me, so many times."

Shushie and I have always shared everything but we've never talked about that until this moment. It was her darkness.

"What made the difference was realising that I am just doing too much caring. I care for mum, I care for Maurice and for Pud caring for Maurice. And then I go into work and people want more of me. They want me to care about them and I do because I can't not. That's who I am."

"Yes, you are wholehearted about everything. I see that," I tell her. "So..?"

A bee buzzes busily by, frantic to collect the nectar it needs while the rain is absent.

"I've thought about this and I'm clear I don't want to stop caring for mum. And I don't want not to be able to help out with Maurice and be there for Pud. So I need to stop having a job that is also about people needing me all day every day and me having to give out the whole time."

"Over-caring."

"Yep. I just want a happy job. Something I can go to and leave behind afterwards, working with people who are well for a while. Not for ever, but for now."

It is not a big revelation. We have spoken of it together recently, and there are no crashing chords as in a momentous turning point to accompany Shushie's words; her decision to leave behind a career of almost four decades. But it is quietly significant, this moment of the third 'c' – choice, where Shushie is choosing to save her own life by recognising and honouring her own needs.

Resistance really is useless

"And you?" she turns to me. We are on a roll now, rocking through these sunlit woods, footsore yet also lighter than we've been for so, so long.

"When we started out, and it's not easy to admit, I suppose thinking about what might happen to change things, I meant us no longer being carers." I don't go so far as to use the D word – mum's.

"I mean I thought the shifts, whatever might happen, would be in the physical world. In our circumstances. When actually what's changed is much bigger and more significant than that."

It's hard to find the words, but Shushie waits for me.

"What's changed is in my mind: all the things that have fallen away, wanting and expecting everything to be a certain way. I don't know how it happened but it's as if I've let go; as if all my resistance to what's happening in our lives has just melted away.

"It's what I teach," I say to Shushie. "That so much of our pain, our suffering, comes not from what happens but from what we think about what happens. Fighting 'what is'.

"And now I know it's true that we teach what we need to learn."

Loving what is

I can't pinpoint the moment the shutters in my mind simply gave way under the pressure of the years, like a rotten shed collapsing in the merest breath of wind. Perhaps hearing myself speak the words that changing our thinking is changing our lives, and recognising finally that changing our minds is sometimes the only choice left to us when the circumstances around us are so far outside our control.

Changing my diet for healthier choices, allowing myself to sleep longer, shedding some work commitments, even saying 'no' once or twice. Like Shushie, understanding that survival means caring for my own needs too.

What I can say is that choosing not to fight 'what is', deciding to accept the way things are, has brought me more peace than I have known for more than a decade. I hear Byron Katie's voice gently asking the simple questions in her book *Loving What Is*: Is it true?

Is it true that all of this caring about everyone else is hard? Sometimes, yes. Certainly every time I have the thought that being a carer is hard I make it harder for myself.

Can you be sure it's true? No, I can't. Because when I let go of the thought that it is hard there is room for me to think it is a privilege to give love and receive gratitude, to be partnering the sister I love with all my heart in this caring and loving, to spend soft time with our childlike mum when all our lives it was hard and she was hard.

How do you feel when you think the thought that it is hard, Byron Katie asks with understanding? Resentful, wrung out, exhausted.

Who would you be without the thought?

I look at Shushie, glowing in the late afternoon sunshine. At the trees reaching skywards, but letting in light pools to the soft green forest floor. At the felltops etched sharp against the blue skyline. We can taste the sweet air.

Nearby, the beck runs through the valley, nosing its way between boulders smoothed by the years, towards the silver lake and beyond it, to the sea we will reach tomorrow.

Every optimistic wildflower is a jewel flanking the path which continues wide and straight and bright ahead.

It has all been here, this beauty and change and peace, all the time. It always will be.

And all we ever need to do is remember that the real journey happens *within*, and move to another place in our minds.

Chapter 28: Skin and blisters, Ennerdale – St Bees

And so we came to the end.

The final day of our Coast to Coast crossing, with the sun high in the sky, the countryside at its overblown lushest: fields ripening and a football World Cup injecting carnival into every humdrum corner.

All we have to do is walk the final 14 miles from Ennerdale Bridge to St Bees.

We'd passed this way before of course. But both of our previous Coast to Coast endings were characterised by dragging boots and sea frets reflecting the fear in us that we might never come back and if we did might never experience the walk in such a glorious spirit of sheer, exuberant discovery.

Now we know we can always return. We've done so. And that makes *this* final morning entirely different: as fresh, buoyant and full of promise as we ourselves are. After our conversations of the previous day this is no reluctant letting go but a spring into the first day of the rest of our lives.

And, at last, the weather colludes.

Arcadia in miniature

The day's first gift, as we climb up out of Ennerdale Bridge, is the surprising discovery of a stretch of moorland, sheep cropping the springy grass, trees low with that ancient blown look of the exposed.

It feels like a closing bracket, reminding us of where we started, looking out over the North Yorks Moors, 15 months and almost two hundred miles earlier.

But this strange patch of Cumbrian moorland is only a minor aberration, and shortly our path takes us off the fell road and down into the unbelievably perfect Nannycatch.

Wainwright calls it an Arcadia-in-miniature and so it is: an unexpected ravine, totally hidden except to walkers, with Nannycatch beck winding beneath the cliff of Raven Crag.

The grazing sheep look a little put out by our arrival, retreating to the cover of bracken and boulders, while small pellets of soft dung reveal the hidden valley's other occupants – rabbits emerging only at dawn and dusk. All around us birds we cannot see sing as if this were the only place on earth.

It's the sort of place to visit with a picnic and no plans but we have plans a plenty and skip through Nannycatch, soaking up its beauty and yet our eyes are peeled for the path that our guidebook promises, or threatens – depending on your point of view – will rocket us skywards for the walk's final climb, up Dent.

'Dear Dent' Wainwright calls it somewhere in recognition of its humble size relative to the Lakeland fells to come. Yet at 1,395 feet Dent is no pushover and, for those on their first Coast to Coast leg, represents an unexpected – and sometimes unwelcome – taste of the challenges ahead.

From the west it presents a long, unrelenting haul to the top where, according to Terry Marsh, the author of our guidebook, 'mere mortals will be obliged to remain in a heap for some time'.

View from the top

Just as well really, as the view from the summit is breathtaking: a panorama out towards the lines of Lakeland fells, across to Sellafield and northwards to the Solway Firth, the twin peaks of the Isle of Man out to sea and, closer, the mound of St Bees Head.

From our direction Dent is a little kinder, offering a forest path that winds upwards in a series of hairpins. It's tough on the legs but we're high on last day adrenaline; so much so that as we emerge onto Dent's grassed summit, we literally burst from the tree canopy like athletes from the blocks.

Well, retired athletes, who are still easing themselves from the blocks as the competition crossed the line. But still, what we lack in speed we make up for in volume, screaming into the breeze 'St Bees here we come'.

We know at the top we'll see our second coast. And so it is: far out there, beyond the patchwork of wide gold and green fields that make up St Bees Head – the opaline blue of the Irish Sea.

It's time for coffee and as we sit I notice something surprising: as much as we love the Lakes, speak of them as 'home', the place where we are most ourselves, on this day we have our backs firmly to the serrated lines of felltops. Instead both Shushie and I look resolutely forward with not an ounce of regret: to where we are going.

A final word on pies

I won't use the word smug to describe how it feels ten minutes later to be flying down Dent, towards the village of Cleator, while group after group slog upwards: stickily red-faced, with barely breath to greet us.

After all, they have 190 miles of magic to look forward to.

But would we swap places with them? No. On this day we're being drawn forward, pulled by the light playing on the distant headland, by the promise of the gulls' cry and sea salt, and by a sense that this time a part of what we are experiencing is a genuine sense of achievement. Reaching St Bees will be a triumph of selfishness over selflessness…and therefore life over existence.

There's nothing to stop for in Cleator. Not even, it turns out, a pie.

(Long story short, there used to be a shop selling pies so big and tasty they become a little legend in their own right. But the Cleator pie maker died and the shop that used to sell them soon after.

The village's other shop has neither the business nous to step into the breach, nor a sense of humour. A large sign outside it reads 'NO PIES'. Trust me on this: we called in for something else they didn't sell and left with a flea in our ears.)

The measly half page in the guidebook given to the final eight miles means we're left to muddle our way through Cleator, eventually deciding to follow a newish cycle track speeding westwards on an old railway line as confidently as the TGV through the French countryside. Another closed bracket perhaps, reminding us of the miles we trekked back at the start with the ghosts of the Rosedale Ironstone Railway as our companions.

After a mile the track heads under a disused railway bridge out into England's summer fields, where even ravenous sheep struggle to keep pace with the countryside's surge skywards. We pass a pond whose waters are entirely hidden beneath reeds growing taller than us, and then on, under another bridge to a track leading to a series of farmhouses whose land this must be.

Occasionally we pass other small groups of Coast to Coasters, and one larger group who seem to be part of an organised trip - perhaps one that has not made it entirely clear the Coast to Coast is a serious walking challenge.

At the front of the trail are a dozen smiling and appropriately dressed Europeans, and, some quarter of a mile behind them, being coaxed forward by the obvious group leader, three Japanese girls dressed for the Arctic and looking as miserable as someone who has walked 180 miles for a famous Cleator pie only to discover the last one has just been sold.

Flying without wings

They are the last west-to-easters we see as we speed out from the fields to farm tracks and then onto a narrow coast road into the pretty village of Sandwith where, on any other sunny Sunday, we might have stopped for a cider on the village green. But still the sea is like a magnet, tugging at us as we bowl along until, in the distance, a clapper board house with a rowing boat stationed in its garden, suggests we're there.

And so it is. To the north, jagged red cliffs and a beach scrubby with seaweed-covered boulders, leading away to the rooftops of Whitehaven. Ahead, a signpost mysteriously encrusted with biting insects. And to the south, and all around us, the promise of a path meandering along the cliff edge, through high grasses and flower-studded banks, smelling of sea and sunshine and the end of our journey.

It couldn't be more perfect; nor a greater contrast from the miles of wet haziness we've slogged through to get to this point.

The fields on the landward side are grown tall with corn while below us white horses bob on a now turquoise sea and the cliffs hold dramas of their own, alive with seabirds of every variety, tucked into shelves and crevices. Other birds ride the breeze effortlessly. It feels as if were we to step off into the blue we'd rise into the air with them.

Full up

We've promised ourselves a picnic on the seacliffs. St Bees won't be our own this time, but no doubt shared with crowds of daytrippers. So, time for reflection must happen before we reach the physical end we decide.

"We'll know the right spot when we see it," I tell Shushie confidently. And we do. A place where the path, running so close to the sheer drop, suddenly takes a 90 degree turn to offer views in both directions, ahead to where we're going, and to our right, far, far, out to sea. There are two large boulders at the junction: no more no less.

Shushie and I kick off our boots and socks and settle in, knowing we can take our time here, in this place where fields and sea and sky meet in a tableau of light and colour and beauty. Where every second a wave unfolding to shore, a bird returning to its young in a cliff crack, or a cloud shadow passing overhead, changes the picture into something new.

After we've eaten, as we sit breathing it all into our souls, Shushie reaches into her backpack for her phone and two sets of headphones. And the vividness of these moments, already being committed forever to memory, lifts to another level with the soaring notes of a favourite anthem: *"I'm coming home again"*.

And fed up

Not everyone is having such a glorious time on the cliff path that day. As we continue to sit in our cliff top perch two youngsters stride by, faces glowing with sunshine, strong legs bare and firm. An older woman huffs after them: "I thought we were going for a walk. Not a route march."

We smile sympathetically at her, assuming her remarks are fond rather than furious. We're wrong. As the young couple wait, her sarcasm turns to a screaming fit. "Let me do this MY WAY. I mean it. Go ahead if you want to go at your own pace. And leave me to mine.

"This is the LAST time I EVER agree to go walking with you."

Ouch. But believe it or not she may not be the angriest walker on the cliffs that day. A few miles on, as the path begins to dip and climb again between the undulations of the velvet fields, another woman, in her middle years, comes towards us –carrying an outsize suitcase.

Bear in mind that we are now several miles from a road in any direction, on a narrow cliff path above a steep drop, where anything larger than a backpack is a liability and distraction. And there she is, dressed for walking, except for the mystery of this massive suitcase which she is alternately dragging behind and shoving with both hands in front of her.

I'd love to be able to give you an explanation but, as we approach, the look on her thunderous face clearly says 'do not even THINK about asking me what has happened and why I am out here alone with enough luggage for a midlife gap year'.

So we don't. But if you're of a literary mind, I might just have offered you a cracking first scene for your next novel.

Journey's end

We've almost reached the end of our story and it's fair to say the closer we come the slower we walk.

We take time out to watch the herring gull fledglings somehow managing to survive on their impossibly precarious perches, while adult birds seem set on dive bombing them to their deaths 200 feet below.

And to take pictures of each other skipping through the fields when, finally, the curve of St Bees beach comes into view.

Here I begin to be at a loss to describe all that we feel as we pick a way down past a vast caravan park to the prom where everyone else is wearing flip flops rather than worn boots - and has that slightly dazed air of day trippers who can't quite believe they are at the seaside and not only is it not raining; it is hot enough to justify an ice cream.

We are separated by distance, both physical and in our minds, and scarcely look at them as we shed boots and socks and allow the sea, its surface glittering with a million diamond lights, to draw us the last few hundred feet. Every step reinforces the separation. Our every nerve-ending is tuned to the feel of warm sand between our toes, to the wailing gulls, the soft breeze tickling our sun-burnished cheeks – and to the shining ocean, calling us home.

Until the wholly blissful moment when our hot, tired feet splash into the waves and we wade as deep as we dare, looking neither to the cliffs we've come from nor the beach behind us. But straight ahead to a horizon etched from liquid silver, stretching as far as our eyes can see.

There are rituals to be performed. Shushie produces a small bottle of champagne from her backpack. And as we gulp its froth we exchange gifts commemorating the journey we've taken side by side, as always.

A long hug seals the moment – our commitment to each other and to continuing our journeying no matter what unknowns the future has in store for us.

It's a damp hug. We're both crying with a mixture of satisfaction, sadness and delight.

You see we have come to the end. And realised it is just another beginning.